CONSTANCE VILLIERS STUART

In Pursuit of Paradise

CONSTANCE VILLIERS STUART

In Pursuit of Paradise

MARY ANN PRIOR

UNICORN

Published in 2022 by
Unicorn, an imprint of Unicorn Publishing Group
Charleston Studio
Meadow Business Centre
Lewes BN8 5RW
www.unicornpublishing.org

ISBN 978 1 914414 43 5
10 9 8 7 6 5 4 3 2 1

Design by newtonworks.uk
Printed in Turkey by Fine Tone Ltd

Frontispiece: detail of Constance Villiers Stuart, **The Hall of
Fountains**, Nishat Bagh, Kashmir, 1912 (see Fig 63)

Page 4: Constance Villiers Stuart, **Statuette and Vase**, c.1930,
watercolour

CONTENTS

FOREWORD   vi

ACKNOWLEDGEMENTS   viii

Introduction   1

CHAPTER 1 Family Background   7

CHAPTER 2 Influences   28

CHAPTER 3 Setbacks   51

CHAPTER 4 An Indian Interlude   78

CHAPTER 5 Preparation and Publication   114

CHAPTER 6 1914–1918: World War I   140

CHAPTER 7 Early Post-War and the Spanish Years   164

CHAPTER 8 Flowers and Finale   206

NOTES   248

BIBLIOGRAPHY   251

INDEX   255

FOREWORD BY THE
MARQUESS OF SALISBURY

Mary Ann Prior is a distinguished art administrator and historian whose expertise has benefited many institutions, public and private, on both sides of the Atlantic. She has now turned her attention to the garden designer, author and artist, Constance Villiers Stuart. Mary Ann Prior lives in Norfolk, as did her subject, so their mutual affection for the county adds to the sympathy the author has for her subject.

And the story is an interesting one.

This country's list of garden designers is rich in formidable women who have strongly influenced the development of horticultural taste. Gertrude Jekyll was the doyenne, but others followed in her footsteps throughout the twentieth century: Vita Sackville-West, Norah Lindsay, Sylvia Crowe, Rosemary Verey, Penelope Hobhouse, to cite but a few. The supply shows little sign of running out during the present century. All of them seem to benefit from being able to combine great knowledge and taste with a formidable quality which complements the individualism and sense of place of the best English gardens.

Constance Villiers Stuart, who died in 1966, was as distinguished as any of them. Although she spent most of her life at her family's house in Norfolk, Beachamwell Hall, she also followed the drum in her early married life. Her husband, an Anglo-Irish soldier, was posted to India, where Constance was entranced by the gardens of the Mughals. She became an authority on the gardens of Islamic rulers from India to Spain, writing about them in two well-received books, painting them, photographing them and lecturing about them. She clearly had a penchant for grandeur, and it was natural that her interest expanded to other equally grand gardens which followed different traditions. Her many articles appeared in glossy magazines, newspapers of record and learned journals.

All artistic endeavour is influenced by other traditions and cultures. Twentieth-century European art owes a great debt to Africa, early Renaissance art to Byzantium, to take two examples. Gardens are no different. China, India, Japan and the Islamic world have all influenced Western European garden design. Within Europe itself, the French had their idea of a 'parc à l'anglaise', and Maria Feodorovna commissioned Charles Cameron to design the park at Pavlovsk with its echoes of Germany and France.

Constance Villiers Stuart had redesigned her own family's garden after a disastrous fire before she went to India. On her return, she, like other artists, was able to bring a broadened susceptibility to her work.

When she died, she left a treasure trove of paintings, sketchbooks and memorabilia which, thanks to the generosity of her granddaughters, is destined for the Garden Museum. It will, therefore, become accessible to garden scholars who will be able to study the contribution that these different traditions and aesthetics have brought to British gardens.

It is curious that this erudite and accomplished woman has hitherto not been more widely known outside specialist circles. In Mary Ann Prior, she has found a Boswell who can put that right in a book whose lavish illustrations and elegant format would surely have appealed to her.

February 2022

ACKNOWLEDGEMENTS

Many people made writing this book an enjoyable experience and were generous with their time, advice and hospitality. I would particularly like to thank Constance Villiers Stuart's granddaughters, Electra May and Aurelia Young, for giving me unlimited access to their grandmother's sketchbooks, paintings, letters, photographs and diaries. They graciously answered my endless enquiries with patience and good humour and were unstinting in sharing their vivid memories of life at Beachamwell Hall. I am indebted to Nigel Hall RA who acted as a catalyst for this book by making the crucial introduction to Electra in 2017. Special thanks are due to my nephew, Gavin Morris, for making my research trip to India in 2019 such a pleasure, and for steering me around various unknown parts of Delhi and Jaipur. I am very grateful to Bill and Jill Husselby for their kindness and support during the past four years.

I wish to thank many others who have helped bring the book to fruition: Julia Stafford Allen, for her help with identifying flowers; Sir Henry and Lady Bedingfeld; Mrs Jane Bonning; Peter Boon and the British Association for Cemeteries in South Asia (BACSA); Giorgia Bottinelli, Curator, Norwich Castle Museum & Art Gallery; David Burnham, Somerset Club, Boston; John Fielden; Paul Frazer, for sharing his transcriptions of letters from Patrick Villiers Stuart and Patricia Nemon Stuart; Ryan Gearing, Unicorn Publishing; Jennifer Glanville, Archivist, University of Reading; Barbara Grubb; Eugenia Herbert; Fred Hohler, Watercolour World; Jane Kennedy, Records Manager, Tate Library; Catherine Longworth; Rollin Kennedy, Unicorn Publishing; Patricia Maitland; designers George and Nick Newton, for the book layout; Dr James Peters, Archivist, University Archive Centre, University of Manchester; Ambrose Robertson, Watercolour World; Georgina Robinson, Archives Assistant, Eton College Library; Daniel Rycroft, University of East Anglia; Alexandra and Crispin Simon, for their hospitality in Mumbai; Catherine Smith, Archivist, Charterhouse School; Ian Strathcarron, Unicorn Publishing; Paul Treacy, Fusiliers Museum; Garry Villiers Stuart; Patrick Villiers Stuart; Rosie Vizor, Archivist, Garden Museum; Jenny Watts, Senior Archivist, Norfolk Record Office; John Wells, University of Cambridge Library; Douglas Wilson; John and Sara Woodall; and Christopher Woodward, Director, Garden Museum.

Introduction

I first came across the artist and writer, Constance Villiers Stuart, née Fielden (1876–1966), when I was travelling in India for research in 2010. With the most well-known of Constance's books, *Gardens of the Great Mughals*, as my guide, I decided to visit Pinjore Gardens in Haryana, mainly because she had painted such a vivid picture of the place in watercolour and words. That she had illustrated the book with her own paintings and photographs struck me as a charming personal touch, and because the book I was clutching had been published in 1913 it also had the allure of a bygone age.

Quite by chance, seven years later, I was invited to a lunch near Beachamwell Hall in Norfolk, where Constance had lived for almost her entire life. As soon as I walked in, I recognised a painting on the dining room wall as the original artwork for an illustration in *Gardens of the Great Mughals*. It transpired that the hostess was one of Constance's granddaughters and that she had in her possession her grandmother's sketchbooks, notebooks, photographs, family correspondence and items of ephemera. The material illuminated her personal life, her travels in India and Spain and her association with newspapers and magazines of the time, particularly *Country Life*. Apart from the framed paintings on the walls, everything at that point was quite muddled and grimy and resided in boxes, suitcases and chests of drawers, or lay hidden away at the back of bookshelves. The contents had been virtually untouched since Constance's death in 1966. When I examined a fraction of the material, it was clear that, except for superficial dust, nearly everything was in good condition. The fact that all these things had lain unseen for so long, and that much of the subject matter seemed at first sight to be disparate and practically unintelligible, made me want to make sense of it and bring it to the attention of a wider audience.

Most of the photographs in the archive were taken by Constance and almost all the watercolour sketches were hers. There was a small collection of sketches drawn by her mother, Frances Fielden, herself a keen and accomplished watercolourist. It was Frances who had encouraged her daughter to take up painting and drawing and had personally tutored her. Constance moved to Norfolk in 1884 at the age of eight and lived at Beachamwell Hall, a 4000-acre estate near Swaffham, for the rest of her life – a long period of residence which kept the archive in one place and ensured its longevity. Despite her desire to keep the estate in the family, it was sold in 1967, a year after her death.

Heiress to a fortune made from cotton production in Lancashire during the Industrial Revolution, Constance, like many of her class, travelled frequently, mostly to the French and Italian rivieras but occasionally further afield to South Africa and Australia. These journeys were made solely out of interest and for pleasure and presented her with many opportunities for painting and exploration. But the only time that Constance left Beachamwell Hall for a long stint abroad was when she went to India in 1911 to accompany her husband, Lieutenant-Colonel Patrick Villiers Stuart, on a military posting of almost three years' duration. During that period, she began exploring Mughal gardens around Srinagar in Kashmir, in Delhi, Agra and other parts of northern India, having decided before she left England to write a book about them. The Villiers Stuarts encountered Lord and Lady Hardinge, the Viceroy and Vicereine of India, at the Delhi Durbar of 1911, and Constance began to communicate with them regularly in an attempt to influence the design of the Viceroy's house and garden which, from 1912, was being planned by Edwin Lutyens and Herbert Baker.

Constance worked as an occasional contributor to *Country Life* from 1914 to 1959, describing for its readers the splendours of Mughal palaces and their paradise gardens, the Moorish gardens of Spain and the great European houses and gardens of Germany, Austria, Denmark, Belgium, Sweden, Holland and France. In 1929 she wrote a second book, *Spanish Gardens*, a hugely successful exploration of the relationship between Mughal gardens and Moorish gardens. Over her long career as a journalist one can trace a waning reliance on watercolour drawing to record what she saw, replaced by a growing use of photography to accelerate her production. This book charts the development of Constance's style of watercolour drawing, which began in childhood and continued to the early 1940s, and the effect that photography wrought upon it, both as adjunct to drawing and alternative means of expression. The latter can best be seen in her heavily saturated colour images of flower arrangements in the 1950s.

No major work has been produced on Constance Villiers Stuart's life or her drawings and photographs. Scholarly studies of Mughal gardens regularly cite *Gardens of the Great Mughals* but there has been no prior attempt at a more in-depth look at the range of her activities. For example, Constance was a leading light in the establishment of the Indian Women's Education Association based in London, which was set up shortly after the First World War to lobby for the franchise for Indian women and to promote girls' literacy at a time when only one per cent of female children in India could read and write. Nor is it widely known that in the 1940s and 1950s she curated, or contributed to, a number of exhibitions of flower and landscape paintings in Norwich and London. Similarly overlooked is her enthusiasm for incorporating more green and open spaces in post-war housing developments in London and other cities throughout Britain. Her promotion of the art

of flower arranging and floral decoration by means of demonstrations, teaching and articles together with her close affiliation with the Institute of Landscape Architects (ILA) are other strands of her life which until now have been unexamined.

When I began to inspect the undocumented and often untitled original photographs and watercolours, the first hurdle in most cases was to discover why they had been made and how, if at all, they related to published illustrations, or if they had been produced solely for personal pleasure. Another task was to determine the various locations depicted in her images. Sometimes it was obvious – for example, a sketch or photograph of the Taj Mahal – but at other times it was not. A random gateway, bridge or fountain might exist in any number of possible sites and seem unidentifiable, but then if one stumbled upon a newspaper cutting or a relevant magazine article and saw a reproduction of the image in question, all became clear, and the discovery allowed a small moment of triumph and satisfaction. At first, writing about the artworks and the woman herself seemed an almost chimerical project because, first, there was almost nothing in the way of secondary sources and, second, the amount of uncatalogued primary material seemed overwhelming.

My approach to the subject has been both broad *and* selective, depending on the available evidence. There was scant information for some aspects of Constance's life, but a superabundance in others. Therefore, I have attempted as best I can to give a broad overview of her background and the major events that marked her career, particularly in the way she adopted a different medium according to the purpose for which it was intended. The book is presented in a narrative and inter-pretive rather than a thematic way. This seemed to be the best approach because so much new and previously unseen material emerged during the course of research that putting it in order and giving it coherent form was, to me, the essential first step, and one which I hope will provide a foundation for future studies. Providing a starting point for more diverse interpretations was a major motivation for resurrecting Constance and her archive from the obscurity into which they had fallen. It is therefore heartening to know that from 2022 all the archival materials will reside at the Garden Museum in London, available to the public.

Finally, Constance lived in an era very different from our own and her attitudes and comments, often racially derogatory and class-bound, reflect that period. From today's standpoint, some of things she said, wrote or did are offensive, even incomprehensible, and very outdated. I have included some of this information, not because I condone it, but to show her in the round, with all her weaknesses as well as her strengths.

Mary Ann Prior
Norfolk, 2022

CHAPTER ONE

Family Background

Constance Mary Villiers Stuart (1876–1966), born Constance Fielden, was a true product of northwest England, situated in its topography and bound by ancestry as well as geography. The first eight years of her life were spent living in the little village of Caton Green, west of the Pennine Chain, from where she and her parents made frequent excursions to the Lake District and the coast around Morecambe Bay. A loving family and proximity to nature formed her first impressions, giving her an idyllic start in life with few, if any, unpleasant distractions. She absorbed every detail of the dramatic surrounding landscape and formed a rich store-house of visual memories and joyful experiences from which she would eventually forge her destiny. Stunning scenery had made Lancashire, Cumberland, Westmorland and Yorkshire fashionable in the eighteenth and nineteenth centuries when poets, artists and writers sought the peace and solitude of the natural world, drawing on it as a source of inspiration. In fair weather, the beauty of the region was unparalleled and the land itself very productive, providing farmers with a decent live-lihood and sustaining local communities over many generations. Yet in winter, the weather could ravage the countryside, transforming it into a hard, bleak, hostile place where aesthetes and tillers of soil alike could quickly be plunged into despair and financial ruin. When Constance Fielden was a child in the 1870s and 1880s, both the spectacular scenery and rural economies were being compromised: industrialisation was well underway, bringing in its wake changes to the appearance of the land and the incomes that derived from it.

For all its many hardships, at least the outward signs of agriculture – its flocks and crops and herds – were picturesque. But as farming became mechanised, agrarian workers redeployed to modern factories and mills to meet the growing demands of new industries, especially cotton and coal production. Technological progress favoured the economy but impinged on the landscape, allowing ugliness to seep in. Huge, dirty, sparsely windowed utilitarian buildings with baking hot furnaces and belching chimneys sprang up along the river valleys, disfiguring everything around them and breaking the health and spirit of the workhands labouring within them. Row upon row of gardenless and blackened terraced houses traced solid curving lines across the landscape like contours on a map, broken at intervals by clouds of figures filtering in for rest, then out again to the monotonous grind and noise of work. As money came rolling in, the fate of nature was of little concern to the ruling classes. Vast fortunes were being created, including a very large one for the Fielden family, until the wealth of the region rivalled that of the South, and made the Northwest an exciting and prosperous place to be. It was claimed, at the peak of the cotton boom, that if Lancashire and its manufacturers suddenly came to a grinding halt then it would ruin the trade of a third of the world, including America, India and all of Britain's existing colonies. During that period of rapid industrial expansion, canals, coal, railways and cotton brought an enormous influx of commerce to the county that it had never seen before, nor has it seen since.

The Fieldens' talent for developing the cotton industry began in the second half of the eighteenth century, when Constance's great-great-grandfather, Joshua Fielden (1748–1811), a full-time yeoman farmer, started buying and selling wool and yarn, and having it spun and woven into cloth for sale in Halifax. Joshua was a man of Quaker origins, blessed with prodigious energy and foresight. He gradually acquired the tenancies, then ownership, of mills along the Calder Valley, but under his aegis production remained small in scale compared with bigger developments in towns like Bolton, Manchester or Preston. It was not until the early nineteenth century that the business really took off, due to the vision and ambition of Joshua's five sons, who took it to the next level and, eventually, to even greater heights, placing it among the top firms of its type in Britain. All the brothers were renowned for their stamina, boldness, enterprise and honesty – traits that would manifest themselves in Constance years later. Sometimes, perhaps out of envy, the Fielden brothers were also called mean, selfish and dour. They were definitely extremely ambitious, expanding production so quickly that they even began to think about sending cloth to Calcutta for the 'mass of poor people'.

Their success took its toll on the ecology of the countryside, but with the enormous profits they made, the brothers bought, managed and preserved enormous tracts of land, amassing a portfolio of country estates and agricultural holdings. In this way, they put something back into the countryside by conscientiously tending and protecting what they owned. Like her Fielden relatives, Constance inherited not just family wealth and characteristics but something intangible – how to resolve the conflict between the modern world of progress and the protection of the built and natural environment. It was a dilemma she would wrestle with throughout her adult life. But at the time, ethical and environmental questions were not preoccupying many people's minds, least of all a privileged child such as Constance. Her first impressions were sensual: feeling the sun, wind and rain on her face, inhaling the scents of field and forest, enjoying wide-open spaces and an amazing variety of sights and sounds. From the family's sumptuous home at Caton Green in the Lune Valley, everywhere around must have seemed to a small girl like one gigantic playground of outstanding natural beauty. Farther afield, familiarity with the Lakes beyond Kirkby Lonsdale, the Yorkshire Dales and the Forest of Bowland, with their impressive peaks, crags, rushing rivers and waterfalls, fostered Constance's great love of nature, particularly flowers and, much later, gardens.

As early as the 1850s, well before Constance was born, her branch of the family had virtually severed itself from direct involvement in the running of the Fielden Brothers cotton business. Her father, also named Joshua Fielden (Fig 1), was one of several heirs to the fortune created by his great-grandfather and expanded by his grandfather and four great-uncles in the early decades of the nineteenth century. The five brothers' families split into distinctive tribes, with four of them known as responsible, upstanding, philanthropic, politically active, civic-minded and stereotypical stalwarts of the community, while Joshua's branch of the family developed in a more wayward direction, acquiring a reputation for being unconventional and individualistic.

Joshua, like other Fieldens of his generation, was connected to the business only through its largesse, receiving a substantial 'income from dividends', as he described his profession in the census of 1881. Whilst the descendants of the family reaped great rewards, they lacked the early Fieldens' creative purpose of changing and, as they saw it, improving the world. Local ties weakened, too, when the Fielden Family Trustees decided that Joshua should be the first in his family to attend Eton College, followed by Magdalene College, Cambridge, where it was hoped he would acquire the polish of a future squire. Although Joshua received a first-class elite education, his achievements were decidedly average, garnering neither distinction nor disgrace. He was apparently pleasant and sociable but lacked the drive to make his mark – he was far happier following instructions than taking the lead. No amount of tutoring could transform him into an energetic go-getter. Besides his absence of ambition and a general ambivalence, there was a mild whiff of controversy that swirled around Joshua's parents, making him reticent.

1   S. Hallé, *Portrait of Joshua Fielden*, 1874, oil on canvas

Born into a strand of the family characterised by independence, even wilfulness, Joshua's life was complicated, something which later impacted on Constance's own life, both propelling her forward and holding her back. Joshua's father, John Fielden (1820–1852) was one of the more bohemian members of the family, completely unconcerned with propriety. He did not care much about public opinion or perpetuating the professional standing of the Fielden brothers; he did whatever he wanted, drank a lot, took the money and lived as a rich outsider. This included seducing the local butcher's daughter, Sarah Cockcroft, when he was in his early twenties. The Cockcrofts were respectable, upstanding tradespeople but Sarah was nonchalant about convention and an independent-minded woman, traits which, along with her good looks, obviously attracted John's attention. They cohabited for several years, during which time they produced two illegitimate children, of whom only one, Mary, survived. Such disregard for conformity displeased the more conservative members of the Fielden family. So, either bowing to pressure or in an attempt to guarantee a secure, reputable future for Sarah, John married her in 1847, a year before she gave birth to their only legitimate child, Joshua. In the 1840s, even though the rigid moral code of the later Victorian period had not yet ousted the more liberal outlook of the Georgian and Regency eras, Sarah and John were an embarrassment for the trustees of the Fielden estate. It was politely suggested that they take their two remaining children and move away from the business stronghold near Todmorden. Not that this request was an onerous one: Greenbank, the house purchased for them on a small estate at Caton Green, almost 60 miles to the west of Todmorden, was quite lovely. Here they were kept out of the limelight in the 'prettiest place in the whole of Lancashire'. Greenbank was kept in the family and was where, in the 1870s, Sarah's and John's son began his married life and where their granddaughter Constance would be born.

As the heir to a very great fortune, Joshua could have risen above petty-mindedness, but instead he was keenly aware of unwelcome interest in his mother's less wealthy background and, as the century progressed, of the growing stigmatisation of illegitimacy. It burdened him to have to keep past events under wraps. This was just adolescent social insecurity, but before then, he had experienced real heartbreak when his father died in 1852, quite unexpectedly, at the age of thirty-two. John had left a young widow to bring up their two children, of whom Joshua, despite being just four years old and the youngest, would inherit the majority of his father's estate. However, his mother and his sister, Mary, had been adequately provided for, affording the fatherless family a comfortable existence and financial stability. What could not be replaced was John's strong, gregarious and unusual personality, making the impact of loss very profound and enduring.

One of the significant assets which Joshua acquired when his father died was the Beachamwell Hall Estate in Norfolk, which in the years to come would play an important role in his and his family's life and become the place to which Constance would form the greatest attachment. In the meantime, when Joshua was nineteen, his mother remarried into another well-known Lancastrian family, the Pilkingtons, an arrangement which secured her lifelong emotional and material well-being. Not much is known about Sarah, but her demeanour and appearance are revealing (Fig 2). In her portrait she exudes the self-confidence of someone who has gained effortless entrée into two of the richest manufacturing families in England and who is wholly at ease with her elevated status. Dressed in a blue velvet dress trimmed with white lace, Sarah boldly confronts the viewer, or the artist himself, with a flirtatious, winsome smile. She exudes an aura of self-possession and appeal that transcends any reservations a man could possibly have about her background. Interestingly, when Constance was an adult (and a renowned snob), she was particularly proud of her paternal grandmother, whom

2   Unknown, ***Portrait of Sarah Fielden***, c.1860,
oil on canvas

she admired for having used her beauty and personality to raise her standing in society.

As Joshua grew up, he showed no great desire to move to the Norfolk estate which he had inherited but not visited. He liked the North, enjoyed the friendly, down-to-earth, straightforward people and felt thoroughly rooted in the region. After university he returned, not to Greenbank, which had been leased out after his mother had remarried, but to the Pilkington family home, Lostock Grange, near Bolton; it was while living there that he fell in love with a local woman, Frances Thom. Throughout his entire life, Joshua avoided making decisions; more often than not, they were foisted upon him. But when he finally settled on Frances as his future wife, he made one of the best choices of his life.

Frances (Fig 3) was born in 1850 not far from Manchester, across the River Irwell in Salford, then an insalubrious town known for brewing and textile finishing trades like dyeing and bleaching. When Frances was a baby, the whole area was burgeoning but dirty, unhealthy and over-crowded – a place inhabited mainly by factory workers living in insanitary conditions. Large families were forced to squeeze into terraced houses built eighty to an acre and made grimy and depressing by industrial pol-lutants. Frances was fortunate: she came from an affluent, well-educated family based just outside Salford in Pendleton, some distance from the worst industrial filth. It was here where her father, John Thom, and his brother David established a soap manufacturing business and, later, a bleaching and dyeing factory.

This was the setting where Frances developed lifelong interests, ideas and views – which eventually percolated down to Constance – as well as a strong personality and presence which loomed large over her daughter later in life, mostly in positive ways. Frances's town and country back-ground and her forceful nature offer clues to how some of Constance's dominant qualities came into being. Like the Fieldens, the maternal side of Constance's family was entrepreneurial, but it was also highly

3   Unknown, **Portrait of Frances Fielden**, c.1870,
albumen print

cultured. Unlike the Fieldens of the same period who were the bene-
ficiaries of their forebears' endeavours, Frances's father and uncle were
innovators trying to get a new business off the ground. Constance leaned
more towards the Thom family's interests, yet the business acumen
common to both her Fielden and Thom ancestries completely passed
her by.

The Thom brothers were originally from Lanarkshire in Scotland;
both attended Glasgow High School, then John went on to study
classics, medicine and chemistry at the University of Glasgow and
Anderson's University.[1] After graduating, he found employment in
northwest England and attained eminence as a highly successful chemist
and dyestuff trader. As soon as he could, John moved his wife, Mary
(née Peet), and his children away from Pendleton and the soap business
to the more wholesome air of Birkacre on the River Yarrow. There he
was invited to be a partner in the Birkacre Company, one of the best
calico printing and bleaching works in Lancashire. Already in large-
scale production when he joined, his science background and talent for
commerce proved a winning combination and, under his management,
the enterprise became even larger and more innovative. He can also
take credit for being a pioneering environmentalist and philanthropist
employer, taking steps to curb pollution and improve factory conditions
for workers. In his obituary, the *Chorley Guardian* stated:

> [John Thom] … sought to keep the streams clear of
> polluted matter and arranged at his works a system of the
> precipitation by means of tanks, which was afterwards
> adopted by others. His kindly disposition led him to take
> much interest in the welfare of his work people and his
> poorer neighbours.

John and Mary gave their children an excellent upbringing. One
of Frances's siblings, Harry, died in infancy, but the other ten children

survived to adulthood and were fortunate in having their natural talents recognised and enhanced by a classical education, including long periods abroad to study foreign languages. Considering the mid-Victorian era in which they lived, John and Mary were progressive, believing in equal education for women and wanting the same advantages for their daughters as those enjoyed by their sons. Mary herself was a well-known harpist, described by John Chatterton, harpist to Queen Victoria, as the best amateur harpist he had ever heard. According to one of her sons, Alfred, she took a keen interest in animals and her garden: 'she … thinned the grapes, pruned the vines and peaches, superintended all the gardening and saw to the numerous pets'. Mary expected all four of her daughters to fulfil their academic potential, and she made sure they were refined by the arts and had an understanding of the natural world. As a teenager, Frances was sent to boarding school at Culcheth New Hall in Bowdon, a prosperous rural hamlet fifteen miles south of Manchester. The school was home to about fifty girls, aged between eleven and eighteen. Culcheth New Hall was recognised at that time as an academic hothouse, attracting gifted pupils from Yorkshire, Lancashire, Middlesex, Scotland, North Wales, Germany and France. It enforced high standards of conduct and intellectual rigour, which Frances, who was clever and able to take lessons in her stride, found easily attainable.

Like several of her siblings, notably Robert, Alfred and Isobel, Frances was artistic, which was a fashionable quality among the leisured classes but also a genuine family interest. Some of the Thom offspring painted miniatures; others made etchings or filled sketchbooks with drawings in pencil and watercolour. They were encouraged by their father to be observant and to experiment with colour, which they happily did, gaining invaluable insights from his own professional knowledge of the full spectrum of natural and synthetic colours. As someone who had turned down the offer of a job as a botanist in India when he left university and who was a close schoolfriend of the explorer Dr David

Livingstone, John Thom was able to explain the colonial origins of many natural dyes. Among these were *Indigofera*, native to India, which produced the much sought-after indigo blue and ultramarine dyes, and the insect-derived colours, like carmine, sourced from cochineal beetles in America. His expertise in chemistry meant he was also extremely well informed about the contemporary race to produce artificial colours, such as mauveine (later known simply as mauve), for the Birkacre Company's rapacious clients in the fashion industry; he understood how dyes were created and the enormous profits brand new colours could earn. Under John's supervision, his children's interest in art went beyond aesthetics to being incorporated into lessons in chemistry and nature. Additionally, art brought wonderful health benefits – fresh air and exercise – as the young Thoms roamed freely around the countryside looking for suitable vantage points from where they painted for entire days *en plein air* (Fig 4). The Thom family's knowledge of colour, fashion, nature and art filtered down the generations, and they became subjects of enduring interest to Constance.

When Frances met Joshua Fielden, she was living with her parents at Burgh Hall, part of the Birkacre estate. It was an unostentatious, yet smart, family home which had the added distinction of having once been owned by the inventor and industrialist, Sir Richard Arkwright. Most importantly, this 'nice old house with a good walled garden [and an] orchard' was just fifteen miles from Bolton, where Joshua's mother and stepfather lived. So, not surprisingly, at some point the young couple's paths crossed. It is not known exactly how their social lives intertwined, but having similar family backgrounds meant they had a lot in common; both had grown up as privileged, sophisticated children of textile celebrities and we can assume that, in this particular close-knit community of successful industrialists, everyone knew anyone of any repute. In one of Frances's early sketchbooks there is a small, undated, unfinished pencil sketch of a reclining man, unmistakably Joshua, in an informal, relaxed

4   Frances Fielden, **Lancashire Landscape**, c.1870, watercolour

pose reading the newspaper. On the opposite page there is a watercolour drawing of a rose with maidenhair fern – symbols of femininity, purity and innocence – dated 1873, indicating, assuming the sketch was made at a similar time, that Frances and Joshua were well acquainted by the early 1870s.

The couple were married at St George's Church in the centre of Chorley on 24 June 1875. Frances was 'superbly attired in a dress of rich white silk, trimmed with Brussels lace, with a tulle veil and orange blossom'. The newly married Fieldens went on a long honeymoon away from the North West, spending time in Devon, Cornwall and London. At the end of the trip, before returning to their new home on the Greenbank estate, Joshua and Frances went to Beachamwell Hall (Fig 5) near Swaffham, in Norfolk, for their wedding feast. There were no immediate plans to move there, but it is clear they had the Hall in their sights as a future permanent residence. With over 4,000 acres, the estate was far larger than Greenbank, the house bigger, architecturally more impressive and closer to London. Joshua and Frances were young, glamorous, rich and social so, naturally, they wanted to be at the centre of things, raise their status, and to be seen and known in society. Beachamwell Hall was an ideal spot for entertaining the county set on a large scale. It was also well placed for establishing their presence in town.

The Fielden Trustees had made a lucky, rather than shrewd, investment when they bought Beachamwell Hall. They could not have known in 1851 how fashionable Norfolk would become over the next few decades. Fortunately for the Fieldens' property values, Queen Victoria gave the county a huge boost and added cachet when, in 1862, she bought the nearby Sandringham Estate as an engagement present for her son, the pleasure-loving Prince of Wales, later King Edward VII. Invitations to Sandringham were naturally a dream goal for the recently married and rapidly gentrifying Mr and Mrs Fielden. In the meantime, over a few gloriously sunny days in late July 1875, Joshua and Frances

5   Unknown, Beachamwell Hall, *c.*1885, silver gelatin print

merely inspected the village, introduced themselves to the tenant farmers and held a banquet for friends and family to celebrate their union. They made a point of marking the end of their honeymoon with a grand flourish befitting Joshua's rank of aspiring establishment grandee and benevolent landlord.

The Fieldens' longed-for baby was born at home at Greenbank on 8 August 1876, amid much rejoicing and deep personal satisfaction for Frances. Joshua was happy too but, ominously, he had begun to show signs of dissatisfaction by drinking too much, bemoaning his lack of purpose and expressing pessimism about his direction in life. At this stage, it was nothing major, but the warning signs of general disillusionment were apparent. Constance was a welcome distraction, eulogised from the outset by Fielden and Thom relatives streaming through the house, as this extract reveals:

> Papa [John Thom] thinks she is like Jos but I think she is more like her mother. She is quite plump, and has dear little velvety cheeks, hands and feet. Her eyes are blue, and she has long dark lashes. Her little nose is quite shapely and Father thinks it will be Roman. This morning she is wearing a swell lace robe to hold a reception for her grandmother … She really is the most wonderful specimen of humanity that ever existed.

Another relative commented that Constance was 'such a pretty little creature, quite a prize one! You can see directly that she is a little girl, not at all mongrel looking.' Materially, this privileged baby would not want for anything and emotionally, too, she was secure, blessed with strong family bonds and the affection of parents who were determined to give their child the very best start in life.

Having undivided attention from nurses, governesses and family made Constance precocious and demanding but, equally, rewarding and charming. She was an intelligent, nice-looking child who could read well, write neatly and make pleasing conversation with adults before she was five years old. She was also very spoilt. Further lustre was added to her exalted image by expensive clothes; Frances insisted that Constance be always immaculately dressed (Figs 6 and 7), in outfits of velvet and lace, pure cotton and silk, topped off with fabulous beribboned hats. She instilled in her daughter a lifelong fondness for couture which only increased in extravagance over the years. Denied little, surrounded by admirers and regularly praised, Constance developed an unshakeable, rock-solid self-confidence. Even her polite little juvenile notes hint at latent adult preoccupations: nature, formality and society. Around 1881 she wrote: 'Dear Auntie, Are your hens quite well? I am sorry I can't send the kitten sooner. Did you enjoy the ball?' And to her mother: 'Dear Mother, I hope you are having pleasant moments. I nearly know the Owl and the Pussy Cat.' By the time she was seven years old, her hand writing was as elegant as an adult's and easily legible. She had begun to insert French words into her sentences e.g., 'My "cheveux" were washed on Saturday'.

When in Lancashire, mother and daughter spent a lot of time in each other's company. Frances was not at all a distant mother, but she did conform to the child-rearing rules of her class and delegated care as a matter of course. When together, they went for long walks, drives and train rides. Constance watched, engrossed, while Frances painted pictures to educate and amuse her. Lengthy separation occurred only when Frances and Joshua went abroad to help him 'recuperate', that is, abstain from alcohol. Even then, Frances employed an army of helpers to look after her daughter and corresponded with her frequently.

Like all young children, Constance exhibited family traits. From her father she gained a sense of absolute entitlement to wealth. Only later would she become aware that her branch of the Fielden family was not the most dynamic and that some among them had been, in her view,

6   J. E. Mayall, *Portrait of Constance Fielden*,
c.1882, albumen print

7   J. E. Mayall, *Portrait of Constance Fielden*,
c.1886, albumen print

8   Constance Fielden, *Study of Flowers*, 1884, watercolour

dangerously self-destructive and non-conformist. Not only had her grandfather, John, fathered two illegitimate children before marrying their mother, but her great-grandfather, an earlier Joshua Fielden (1778–1847), had also had an illegitimate child, with a young mill-hand, before settling down to a conventional marriage with another woman. This particular Joshua was known to carouse wildly and favour enjoyment over employment, being, just like his son and grandson, interested only in the handsome profits generated by Fielden Bros and not at all in how the company functioned. Constance inherited her mother's love of nature, gardens and flowers, painting and history, which was coupled with the same assurance, drive, determination, razor-sharp focus and will of steel as her innovative, eighteenth-century Fielden forebears. By the time Constance was seven or eight years old, the die was cast and the foundations for her lifelong interests were firmly established. She had already produced the first of the many signed paintings of flowers that she would make over the course of her lifetime, a small study in water-colour dated 1884 (Fig 8).

CHAPTER TWO

Influences

Towards the end of the nineteenth century, travelling abroad became an obsession in the Greenbank household. Joshua and Frances regularly left the country, often for as long as two or three months, especially in the winter. Constance remained at home with a nurse, a housekeeper and other domestic staff along with various visiting uncles and aunts, while Frances, Joshua and older members of their immediate family went away.

Frances usually kept a journal during these trips, but only rarely does she mention Constance. Not that this is particularly surprising because, at the time and in their social strata, it would have been unseemly to let babies and children impinge on one's normal way of life and being worried about them or preoccupied with them would have indicated misguided priorities. What Frances's journals do provide are occasional insights into the attitudes and opinions of the people with whom Constance was growing up. It also illuminates one family's personal experience of an expanding tourism industry which enabled the middle and upper classes to broaden their mental and physical horizons. Just like their aristocratic predecessors on The Grand Tour over a hundred years earlier, cultural tourists of the late nineteenth century went abroad to acquire sophistication, knowledge and status following the same well-trodden paths, but covering the distance in a fraction of the time. Frances and Joshua wanted condensed cultural experiences; thanks to the growth of rail and steamship travel, they could pack all of them into two or three very comfortable and enjoyable months. The deluxe, highly curated travel patterns established by her parents gave Constance an enticing blueprint to replicate in the following century. She even surpassed them, travelling farther afield, for longer and at much greater cost.

As a young child, Constance would not have been especially interested in her parents' travels, although she might have gleaned some idea of how much they had enjoyed their extended holidays from listening to their enthusiastic descriptions. It would not be until 1888, when Constance was thirteen and considered suitably civilised, that she would be allowed to join her parents on a long-distance voyage. Before then, Frances and Joshua continued to follow travel trends, decamping to the chicest resorts in Europe – Cannes, Menton, Nice and Bordighera – places which were becoming increasingly popular with elite British tourists during the colder months. While she was away, Frances painted local flowers (Fig 9) and landscapes (Figs 10, 11 and 12) in bold colours and an assured style, to share with Constance when they were reunited. Together they would pore over these pictures, while Frances added vivid commentary and anecdotes to whet her daughter's appetite for art and travel.

In the early 1880s, overseas travel was temporarily suspended while the family made decisions about where they were going to live. The lease on Beachamwell Hall and its farms expired in 1881, and the sporting rights, then leased to Lord de Clifford, were due to expire at the end of 1884. Even though Joshua had reservations about moving his family from a county where they had roots and reputation to another where they had neither, it was the ideal moment to relinquish Greenbank to a tenant and fulfil the promise made on their honeymoon to make Beachamwell Hall their main residence. It was always going to be an upheaval to leave a wide network of Northern friends and relatives for a life among strangers on the other side of the country, and Joshua

9   Frances Fielden, *Flower Study 2: jonquil, blue wood anemone (anemone blanda), red garden anemone (anemone de caen), mimosa and purple violet (viola)*, 1884, watercolour

10   Frances Fielden, *Île St. Honorat*, 1882, watercolour

11   Frances Fielden, **St Marguerite**, 1884, watercolour

12   Frances Fielden, *Village near Castiglione*, 1882,
watercolour

and Frances wondered anxiously how they would they be received in Norfolk.

Relocating south was also a wrench for Constance; she missed her extended family, including Lancastrian cousins and children of a similar age, and was lonely in Norfolk. Having a home tutor made it more difficult to socialise, but Frances worked assiduously to connect her daughter with the children of prominent families in the area, some of whom would become lifelong friends. Among these were the inhabitants of grand mansions, mostly larger and more historically distinguished than her own: Oxburgh Hall, Narborough Hall, Hillington Hall, Stradsett Hall and, farther afield, Didlington Hall and Elveden Hall, then owned by Maharaja Duleep Singh. Constance formed a friendship with the Maharaja's daughter, HH Princess Bamba who, later in life, would prove to be an invaluable resource for information about the rituals and customs of Mughal and Sikh gardens.

The transition went ahead smoothly in early 1885, and the Fieldens discovered just how perfect Beachamwell Hall was for a young family. It was spacious, well proportioned, comfortable and attractive yet imposing, with many amenities like stables, paddocks and tennis courts. Although the gardens had been thoroughly neglected, they offered an enticing opportunity to create glorious borders, rockeries and flowerbeds. Beyond the gardens lay acres of parkland, farmland and the pretty village of Beachamwell. The family was not daunted by so many interior and exterior projects; instead, they were excited and keen to personalise their home and get immersed in running the estate. Lord de Clifford held an auction of his belongings in January 1885 to offload a miscellany of high-quality furniture, plated goods, linen, china, glass, carriages, harnesses, two horses, fifty-three fowls, and the gamekeeper's and gardeners' effects. Joshua and Frances eschewed the livestock, but they thoroughly enjoyed skimming off the cream of the peer's surplus possessions to take back to the Hall. It was fun and thrilling to be making their mark on a new home.

Another important motivation to move south was Joshua's appointment as High Sheriff of Norfolk in November 1883. He had had no hesitation in accepting and commencing his term of office in March 1884 because not only was it an honour, but it was also a way of elevating himself and overcoming the stigma of 'being in trade'. The nomination implied that, whatever the source of an appointee's wealth – within reason – he was indubitably a man of integrity and good breeding, and therefore a role model for the community. Joshua could not claim centuries of titled, landed ancestors, but he fulfilled other criteria: he was extremely rich, he owned extensive acreage in Norfolk as well as an estate and some working mills in Lancashire which accrued substantial income from rents and dividends. These attributes gave him social credibility and being raised to the dignity of the office of High Sheriff significantly embellished his public standing.

Becoming High Sheriff gave Joshua a taste for Norfolk life; he liked and respected the people he had met there over the course of 1884 and felt a greater sense of belonging. Moving to Beachamwell Hall proved beneficial for everyone, although in the long term the benefit was greater for Frances and Constance than for Joshua. Any lingering insecurities they may have had about their place in county society were firmly quashed when the Fieldens received their first invitation to Sandringham in January 1885, sent on behalf of the Prince of Wales, who was holding a ball to celebrate his coming of age. This definitely augured well for the family as they commenced a new life on their own terms, away from the insular communities of the North.

Frances and Constance shuttled between Norfolk and Lancashire for two years after the move, as did a stream of Fielden and Thom relatives. Family ties were strong, and letters between Frances and her siblings criss-crossed the country almost daily, often with little to say; yet the mere fact of making contact said so much. Nature notes – gardens were a frequent topic – vied with health and money for space in the almost illegibly scribbled lines written vertically and horizontally across the page. On one of her first return visits to the North, Frances painted some tiny (8.9 cm × 12.7 cm) nostalgic sketches of Lancashire beauty spots, executed with charm and delicacy (Figs 13, 14 and 15), perhaps in an effort to keep homesickness at bay.

Joshua and Frances resumed foreign travel in 1887. They chose Egypt, but there was now a big difference between this journey and their previous ones, because Constance, aged ten, was able to engage in a lively and intelligent correspondence. This cache of letters shows that, within the emotional constraints of the day, Frances and Joshua doted on their daughter to the point of overcompensating for their absences. She was always 'our own darling' or 'my Precious Lily', evidently perpetually in their thoughts (despite these sometimes being tinged with guilt). Frances repeatedly wrote: 'I do hope you are happy'; 'it seems a very long time since I saw you on the step as we drove away from Beachamwell'; and 'It's so bitterly cold that I felt happier to think you were at home where you would have a warm, comfortable room.' They fussed over her health, which seems to have been delicate. They promised visits to Crystal Palace, trips to the seaside, copious treats and presents when they returned. Frances hoped her absences would not overly affect her daughter, but actually Constance was upset about being left behind in the care of Miss Bovay, her French governess. Nevertheless, she emulated and perpetuated the model of intermittent parenting several decades later. What Constance had experienced as a child helped her, as an adult, to justify more frequent and longer absences from her own child.

Even if Frances had wanted to hurry back to Constance, it would have been difficult. During the 1880s, long-haul journeys were still slow, and the outward and return journeys consumed a large portion of an expedition. Just to sail from London's Albert Docks to the mouth of the Suez Canal took twelve days. Joshua, Frances, her father and her

13   Frances Fielden, **Rocks at Heysham**, *c.*1885, watercolour

14   Frances Fielden, **Wharton Crags**, *c.*1885, watercolour

15   Frances Fielden, **Harrock Hill**, c.1885, watercolour

sister Marion set off on the SS *Tasmania* on 10 February 1887, sailing non-stop to reach Port Said on 22 February.

Since 1882, Egypt had been a British protectorate, and Frances's travelogue is written from an unabashedly Orientalist standpoint, seeing people through the prism of Anglo-Saxon superiority over not just the Egyptians, but most of the world. To her, it was perfectly natural that Egypt, like India, should be 'modernised' and brought under the control of the British because 'all these places on the Nile are much safer since the English came than they used to be'. Constance absorbed the idea that British norms should be universal, and that her homeland's 'civilising' values improved and elevated other nations.

Frances expressed her opinions about Britain's place in the world, echoing the dominant views of her era. For instance, Frances was against the practice of slavery, finding it absolutely abhorrent. She wrote to Constance that she and Marion had ridden 'very fast' donkeys through the crowded bazaar at Assiut, noting that it had once been a slave market but 'happily that has now stopped'. The steamer kept side saddles on board for European tourists because, according to Frances, 'in these queer places there are no side saddles'. Even with the right tack, they admitted to feeling nervous about being thrown from their mounts in the narrow market passages as they trotted past camels bearing very wide loads. They sometimes rode out of the town and into the hills to inspect rock tombs: 'a horrid sight [where] there were quantities of pieces of mummies and the cloths they had been wound in lying about the hillside'.

Shortly afterwards, having a few days of leisure in Cairo, Frances composed long letters to Constance containing information about haggling ('not at all like our English way and I don't like it'), clothing and religion (Fig 16):

> Over the nose, the peasant women wear a gold or brass
> ornament which looks like three large thimbles stuck

16   Unknown, **Arab Women, Port Said, Egypt**, 1889, albumen print

one inside the other … Heads are always covered with
the dark blue dress. Across the lower part of the face the
women wear a black veil fastened to the nose ornament
and hanging down below the knees. … Friday is the
Mohammedan Sunday; Saturday is the Jews' sabbath.
Sunday is the Christian sabbath so there are three
Sundays in a row in Cairo. We were very glad to go to the
English Church last Sunday and hear our own service.
There are so many different nations in Cairo – people
from so many other countries. It is always interesting
watching [them passing] to and fro. … there are many
languages. In the shops they speak English, French,
Italian but in the bazaars (chief buying places) they speak
Turkish, Arabic and Persian.

There are frequent instances of Frances writing about foreigners,
which are relayed more in astonishment than hostility, but always
viewed from a sense of otherness. On the outbound journey, leaving
England, she had sent Constance a description of the people she was
travelling with:

There are about 60 passengers on the Tasmania and
several children. Some of them are going to live in India
and one family of six are going to Japan. Their home is in
Japan – they have … been to England, some of them on
a visit and the bigger ones to school. They have a Chinese
nurse – such an odd-looking woman in regular Chinese
dress. Her feet seem to have been squeezed away when
she was a baby and she goes about as if on stumps. Her
Chinese slippers are something like dolls' slippers, very
pointed with no room for toes and only a broad heel and
bandages instead of stockings on her feet.

Frances was even more surprised when she learned that the children in the care of the Chinese nurse had their own cow on board to ensure they had adequate milk for the journey.

Of the crew, she wrote:

> There are 150 in number; half are Indians and Ethiopians.
> All very smart in <u>clean</u> white trousers, white cotton coats
> or shirts and very gay sashes. Some shirts are made of very
> fine muslin, some of very fine silk. On heads [they wear] an
> embroidered cap with a scarlet turban twisted round and
> the short end falling at the back. ... they all had bare feet.
> It looked odd to see all the toes in a line – they all had just
> to touch one division of the boards on deck so it was a very
> straight line.

From correspondence and travel notes, it is clear that what was being communicated to Constance by her mother echoed what would have been expressed and endorsed in conversations at home: an entitlement to luxury; the right to access select networks; a belief in imperialism, monarchy and British superiority; and the subordinate place of children within the family.

Finally, in 1888–1889, it was time for Constance to take part in a journey to the colonies. For a child who was at last to be included in an adult trip, it was a very exciting adventure, one which Constance had anticipated for months, and which would fulfil all her expectations. The choice of her maiden voyage was as ambitious as it was long – Australia, then regarded as a rapidly developing British outpost for trailblazing gold prospectors and land grabbers who bravely coexisted alongside dangerous convicts and bushrangers. Considering that they were travelling there at the height of a land boom, it is likely that Frances and Joshua were exploring investment opportunities. Ironically, this journey – Constance's debut on the high seas – was one in which the whole family almost died in a near-fatal storm. Frances chronicled the event in a detailed description written on board the *Sobraon*, off Cape Leeuwin, Australia:

> We have been 84 days on the ocean ... we were advised to come by sailing vessel as being much better for the health than a steamer. ... Don't you be persuaded at any time to go by sailing ship – there are so many discomforts and the time is so long. The company is, with only a few exceptions, very commonplace. ... We had a heavy gale on 29th Nov and were all much frightened in the night by a tremendous crash and then a downpour of water. A wave broke on deck and smashed a great part of the skylight. The water was inches deep in the saloon. It was intensely alarming. [The gale which] lasted for three days was of most unusual force. The captain said he had never seen anything like it. We had strong winds and strong currents – the sea seemed to be coming upon us in gigantic waves in all directions. ... people fled horror-stricken.

We learn some interesting things from this voyage: how Constance reacted to danger and setbacks; the state of Joshua's health; and how well, for her age, Constance could paint and draw. Despite a hitherto cossetted upbringing, Constance was surprisingly blasé about the storm: '[she was] not the least bit alarmed and thoroughly enjoyed peeping from her bunk at the excitement. ... and the whole ship life delights her'. It was the same story for the entire time they were away – from October 1888 to May 1889 – Constance was in her element, exploring, spending time outdoors, learning experientially and meeting new people, sometimes incurring her mother's disapproval: 'She has too much her own way and the 2 girls about her own age [with whom she's made friends] are colonials and much more forward than I like in their manners.' Constance's health improved in the heat, dust and storms of the eight-month tour and, contrary to all predictions, she positively flourished, which could not be said of her father. Joshua had grown 'stout' and was begrudgingly 'on the wagon'. Frances seems to have used travelling abroad as a way to ween him off alcohol, which is borne out by her comments: '... he has had many privations and has been teetotal since he came on board. Ginger ale is he thinks the best substitute for beer'; and 'Jos has at times been so wearied by the monotony of life on board that he has repeatedly said he would take the first steamer straight back to England!'

If Joshua was morose, then at least Constance and Frances could console themselves by documenting their journey by sketching, which they had begun doing as soon as they had set sail. It was the first time that mother and daughter had spent such a long, uninterrupted time together; this happy period gave them the freedom to choose subjects they liked, tackle them in their own way and compare the results in each other's sketchbooks. Constance began by having fun with the nautical flag alphabet and the different meanings of each flag expressed through its shape and markings (Figs 17 and 18). The left-hand column of flags depicted in Figure 18 is code for: B (Bravo) = dangerous cargo; D (Delta) = keep clear; P (Papa) = vessel is about to sail; V (Victor) = require assistance. Equally appealing to a child was 'crossing the line' and, on 3 November 1888, on the outbound voyage, they reached the equator. Frances and Constance celebrated the moment by each painting her own version of the *Nancy Smith* of New York crossing at the same time as the *Sobraon*. Their pictures are almost indistinguishable from one another (Figs 19 and 20), although Frances's sketch is a little more subtle, with finer lines and evidence of greater control of the brush; Constance uses slightly bolder colours, but the overall effect is very similar.

Once in Australia, the family spent a few days recovering in Melbourne, during which time they were formally photographed. A foxed and faded

17   Constance Fielden, ***Ship's Flags on Sobraon***, 1888, watercolour

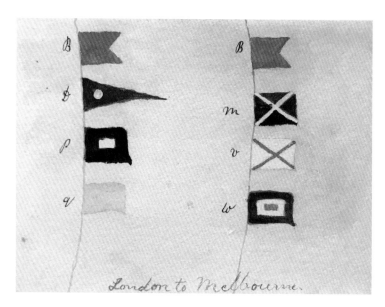

18   Constance Fielden, ***Ship's Flags on Sobraon***, 1888, watercolour

19   Constance Fielden, *The Nancy Smith of New York crossing the Line*, November 1888, watercolour

20   Frances Fielden, *The "Nancy Smith" of New York crossing the Line*, November 1888, watercolour

image renders the sitters ghostly, uncomfortable, almost shell-shocked, possibly as a consequence of having just survived a nerve-wracking sea crossing (Fig 21). Constance and Frances stare directly and confidently at the photographer, while Joshua self-consciously averts his gaze. No one looks happy; nevertheless, the portrait stands as a striking memento of their endurance. Things improved as they started to explore Victoria, New South Wales and, towards the end of their journey, South Africa.

To the northeast of Melbourne lay the Yarra Valley, a region which had begun to attract tourists and speculators in the early 1880s. More visitors arrived every year, and particularly in 1889, when the opening of a railway line extension to Healesville made the area accessible from Melbourne and, therefore, perfect for investment. The Fieldens chose to stay in the vicinity, first at the Grand Hotel, then afterwards at the Healesville Hotel, from where they could visit Mount Riddell, Burgoyne and the Mundi Hills to consider what profits could be made. It is unclear whether they actually bought shares or backed any venture, but unless one had business interests there was not a great deal for a tourist to do in the area apart from making sketches and surveying the landscape. Constance and Frances were most productive during this interlude. From their artistic output, it is evident that the *Nancy Smith of New York* sketches had been misleading, and that there were differences in ability between mother and daughter. Fig 22, showing Mount St Leonard in the background and the clearing for the railway in the foreground, demonstrates Frances's technical finesse and patience, whereas Constance's painting of a bush fire on the Mundi Mountain range (Fig 23) shows youthful impatience in her rapid application of paint and the hurried scrawl of the inscription. Between the two of them, they filled their sketchbooks with a total of about thirty-five watercolours, including some which were painted in Adelaide, and others in Algoa Bay, in the Eastern Cape of South Africa, where they stayed on the way back to England. Constance's sketchbook from Australia is her earliest one in

21   F B Mendelsohn & Co., *The Fielden Family*, 1889,
albumen print

22   Frances Fielden, **Mount St Leonard from the balcony,**
Healesville Hotel, 1889, watercolour

23   Constance Fielden, *Bush Fire in the Mundi Ranges*, 1889, watercolour

existence, and it shows evidence of having had some instruction either from her mother or a drawing master, or both. She was already having dancing, music and singing lessons in addition to her academic studies, so it is highly likely that she was being taught drawing as well.

The voyage to Australia had taken too long for the Fieldens' liking. No doubt Joshua and Frances had wanted, for Constance's sake, to make this the most exciting trip imaginable by going as far away from England as possible, for as long as possible. It had not worked, and they never travelled such a long distance by sea again. Whilst it had not been an enjoyable expedition for her parents, Constance had loved it, and from then on was gripped by wanderlust. Thanks to her mother's influence and her own experience of sailing to Australia, the idea of a romantic nomadic life painting, writing and visiting far-off lands had firmly taken root.

CHAPTER THREE

Setbacks

Beginning in 1890, the Fieldens' lives went sour. They endured more than a decade of intermittent misery in which events conspired against them. These years cast a long shadow over Constance's hitherto untroubled life, leaving her sadder and more wary, but tougher. Many of the character flaws for which she was criticised later in life – rigidity, snobbishness, wilfulness, ruthlessness, pretension – may have had their origins in the difficulties of this period. By contrast, adversity magnified her strengths: her intellectual curiosity, clarity of purpose and determination to succeed all came to the fore.

There were minor incidents, such as their butler, John Coombs, regularly stealing jewellery from Frances and trying to impute the thefts to the housekeeper. When the case went to court, the 'rapacious and untrustworthy' Mr Coombs (alias Roberts), was labelled by the judge as 'of the dangerous class'. Considering the butler had been living with the Fieldens for several years, this description was highly alarming. Then there were other more emotionally upsetting events, such as the prolonged illness of Constance's grandfather, John Thom, and his subsequent death in October 1891. During his illness, regular medical bulletins emanated from the North. In one of them, Frances's sister had enigmatically referred to Joshua, asking if he was 'in fair spirits', adding 'I know you said he had to be so quiet because he could not stand talking', and she had ended by saying 'I am so distressed that you are having two anxieties'. The strain of her father's decline affected Frances deeply and, compounding it all, her husband's health had also begun to be a problem.

Constance had been close to her grandfather. He was a genial, good-hearted, patient and reassuring man who excelled as a correspondent; he often wrote to Constance about country matters, describing farm animals, seasonal flowers, birds and, with particular pride, horses, horse racing and hunting. His sons (Constance's uncles Walter and Alfred) were, like their sisters Frances and Marion, excellent riders who derived great pleasure from their thoroughbreds. Whenever Constance was at Birkacre, she and her grandfather gardened together. Significantly, he fuelled her nascent interest in horticulture by giving her a little plot of land to design and plant. When he was ill during the final year of his life, he wrote to Frances to say that the flowers in Constance's garden were in bloom, noting 'I always think of her and her cousins when I see [the daffodils], which is daily, even when I cannot go there and feel a pleasant jumble of associations of grandchildren, spring, lovely flowers and good gifts of a good God.'

When her grandfather died, Constance was a mature fifteen-year-old with a typical adolescent desire for more freedom and independence. Recognition of this came in the summer of 1892 when she was allowed to travel without her parents to Morlaix, a small town in Brittany, to perfect her French. She was chaperoned by an aunt and uncle but even this represented liberation. Although Frances was not physically present in France, her influence over Constance is clearly evident as their roles reversed, with the mother now at home and the daughter abroad. Frances had written about the appearance and habits of people she had encountered in Egypt, and now Constance composed ethnographic descriptions of Breton costumes and customs to entertain her mother:

> The men's costume here is quite different to Dinan. Instead
> of the long blue blouse they wear short black coats with rows

of small brass buttons and open double-breasted waistcoats with more brass buttons, a white shirt and a bright blue sash round their waist. They have straw sailor hats turned up round the brim with black velvet [trim] and a black velvet band wound with long ends hanging over the hat and a large silver buckle.

Just as Frances had done when she toured Italy and Egypt and bemoaned the infrequency of her painting sessions, Constance also laments the lack of time available for sketching between sightseeing and other distractions. Nevertheless, she manages to illustrate her letter with diagrams of Breton women's traditional caps, adding notes about fabrics, shapes and styles from the everyday to the festive. The Morlaix cap was 'not very pretty' but the Quimper cap (a high one with lots of string), caught her eye. She had tried to draw it but the wearer had moved on: 'On our way home we saw it again and followed her like detectives studying the cap until she turned up a very dark and dirty street.' Constance's keen interest in fashion and appearance spills across the pages in numerous spirited observations:

> Their shawls are the most lovely colours, moss greens, dull blues, greys and reds … The most amusing thing here is to see some of the people dressed in the latest Paris fashions, suede glove s… and caps! … Most of the people wear sabots or go bare-foot … Saw a revue of two cavalry regiments, hussars and dragoons, but I don't think they look half as smart as the Yorkshire … The men look very much alike because they are all clean shaven.

At the time of Constance's visit, Brittany was extremely fashionable and artists, in particular, had great enthusiasm for the region. They were attracted by the rugged, windblown landscape, the sea, the traditional folk costumes, and the ancient language and customs of the inhabitants. Breton women in local dress provided an obvious motif and a lure for French, English and Irish artists including Paul Gauguin, Paul Sérusier, Maximilien Luce, Roderic O'Conor and Stanhope Forbes, among others. The popularity of Brittany was such that an artists' colony formed at Pont-Aven,[2] a little port lying at the mouth of the Aven estuary, in southwest Finistère, some seventy-five miles from Morlaix to the northwest. Constance's artistic eye was similarly drawn to Brittany's distinctive characteristics: the winding, narrow lanes, the beautiful coastal paths and the then relatively modern feat of engineering, the Viaduc de Morlaix. Equally intriguing were the half-timbered 'lantern' houses built in the sixteenth century for members of the aristocracy and wealthy linen merchants, including the Maison de la Duchesse Anne, which Constance described at length to Frances. Above all, however, like the artists of the Pont-Aven School, she was fascinated by the women's costumes.

Brittany was the high point of 1892, but that short and happy interval was completely overshadowed when, two months later, Joshua Fielden died unexpectedly on 22 October, aged forty-four. Constance and Frances were completely stunned and left reeling because, besides the emotional ramifications, there were overwhelming practical matters to consider. Frances had little, if any, experience of running an estate beyond the domestic confines of house and garden, and she wasn't cut out for it. Suddenly, without warning, she was bereft and facing the lonely task of single-handedly maintaining, educating and bringing up Constance 'suitably to her station in life', and of being the sole proprietor of a large house, 4,000 acres of farmland, numerous staff and tenants.

Frances and Constance were fortunate in that they were still rich, having been bequeathed a personal estate of over £27,000 (equivalent to £3.5 million today), and all of Joshua's properties, which amounted to a generous income during her widowhood. Joshua had also stipulated that, upon Frances's death or remarriage, all his real and personal estate were to be held in trust for Constance for life. Although mother and daughter were secure, Frances could foresee a time when their wealth might ebb away due to her lack of experience and the attendant threat of being exploited.

Joshua's death had a lifelong impact on Constance. The immediate shock and grief numbed her and shook her confidence. Where there had once been a mild-mannered, indulgent and loving father, now there was a vacuum at just the time when she most needed paternal advice and guidance. There was a rumour that Joshua had died of alcoholism, encouraged in his habit by a yet another renegade butler who had plied him with drink when he was supposed to be abstaining. It was also suggested that his income had dwindled due to decreased rentals and a downturn in agricultural revenues during the Long Depression of 1870–1893, which had made him anxious, depressed and more inclined to turn to the bottle for solace. There were many theories about what might have contributed to his early death, but no certainties.

Now that the family comprised just two women, Constance must have felt adrift. Yet, she was also tough in extremis. Even in mourning, it is unlikely that she could envisage herself ever falling victim to what she regarded as her father's weaknesses. Perhaps the ambiguous circumstances of Joshua's death hardened her heart because, over time, Constance became a renowned martinet, insisting on the highest standards of conduct, enforcing compliance and refusing contradiction. Specifically, in response to insinuations of alcoholism in the family, she developed an enduring aversion to drink and a loathing of drunkenness. Considering the earlier signs of her vitality and exuberance – the enthusiasm of her sketches in Australia, and the brio of her correspondence from Brittany, in which we can sense how thrilled, happy and excited she had been to be on the threshold of adult life, it was a huge blow for everything to come to a grinding halt when her father died.

Constance needed to complete her education, and in 1894 Frances began looking around for suitable places where her daughter could study. Because she enjoyed art, dancing, history and French, most of those interests could be satisfied by spending time abroad at a reputable girls' school. Frances considered sending Constance to Limoges so that she could be privately tutored by a Monsieur Chahol who taught music and French and ran art classes in association with the École des Beaux Arts. Every September, M. Chahol came to Cambridge and Norwich, armed with glowing recommendations and impressive introductions, to meet a select group of mothers in the hope that, over numerous competitors, they would choose his 'educational salon for ladies' at which to have their 16-to-20-year-old daughters educated. Eventually Frances, no doubt not wanting to live alone, decided to keep Constance at home. So, instead of pursuing further education, Constance spent the next few years helping her mother adjust to widowhood and shouldering a share of running Beachamwell Hall.

Travelling abroad was temporarily out of the question because the family's financial affairs needed to be put in order. A great deal of the Fielden and Thom correspondence in the early years of the 1890s referred to money: how to get the maximum return on investments; which new investments should be made; what income to expect from property sales and rentals; how to plan and whom to trust. Unfortunately, the economy was in recession and there were no signs of a quick recovery – a predicament which badly affected Frances in the short term. She wrote to a Mr Read who had expressed 'willingness to help in the matter of the farms':

> I venture to send you a copy of the terms on which the
> two farms are offered. Mr Clacton Mason draws up the
> particulars of the farms and thought a very low rent with all
> the shooting rights might induce a sporting tenant to farm

the land. The present shooting rent received for these two farms alone is £500 a year. When Mr Fielden took these farms into his own hands, £11,000 was spent stocking them: Shingham £4,000 and Malt House £7,000, ten and six years ago respectively. Since this time a considerable amount of arable has been laid down as permanent cut grass. ... Is it possible you may know of someone likely to take a farm for the sake of exceptionally good shooting?

This letter, just one of several examples indicating Frances's plight, alludes to Joshua's past tendency to overinvest which now contributed to his widow's challenging situation. The news from the North was just as bad. Reporting the annual figures of the Birkacre Company, Frances's brother informed her: 'Our business has done badly since Xmas and everybody else is in a bad way, I fear.' As late as 1902, Frances was still struggling with fundamental estate management and obviously out of her depth. Her friend and neighbour, Sir Alfred Bagge, offered to come to her aid:

My son has horrified me with his account of the way in which you are being 'done' over your property. I propose to ask you a few questions, and if possible, put you in the way of mending things a bit. ... I feel I can't rest and see you swindled. If you have any printed leases (I hope you have) I shall ask you to let me see one. I shall also ask to see your income tax and poor's rate receipts. Your income tax is liable to deductions, but perhaps you may not be aware of it. You ought to be paying Poor Rates on the Hall, Gardens and Cottages (not on cottages let with farmers), plantations and any land you may be occupying as your Home Farm. ... After going into these questions I shall be better able to give you a hint how to alter the present state of affairs.

Constance remained largely unaware of the true state of their financial uncertainty because Frances herself kept up appearances and continued an active social round. By the mid-Nineties they were both attending balls, shooting lunches and dinners across the county, mingling with a fashionable array of guests including the Prince of Wales and his brothers, the Duke of Saxe-Coburg, the Duke of Cambridge and the Duke of York. Others circling in the same orbit were the Maharaja of Cooch Behar, the Duke of Marlborough, the Earl of Pembroke, the Earl Cadogan, the Marquis d'Hautpoul, the Marquis of Waterford and Sir William Ffolkes. House parties were held at Beachamwell Hall, where far-flung members of the family were invited to meet guests such as fellow Northerner Frank Hird, a journalist and author of books about Lancashire as well as, controversially at the time, being the lover of Lord Gower; others included Margaret Fountaine, a lepidopterist and amateur scientist who lived at Norwich, the future naval commander Chichele Keppel Hart and the eminent garden historian, Alicia Amherst.

Their world was opening up again, and it was around this time, too, that they resumed travelling, enabling Constance finally to study art in Rome and Paris. It is not known whether her artistic training took place in a formal setting or whether it was more haphazard. Following the deaths of John Thom and Joshua Fielden, the first trip which Constance and Frances made to Italy seems to have had an educational component, and some of the sketches made there in 1895 indicate that Constance was having drawing lessons. Copying casts and architecture was then common practice for students despite this type of classical, technical instruction waning and being replaced by a looser, more spontaneous style of drawing. While on their three-month-long tour, the two women put in a brief stop at Salerno, a city interesting to them as the Italian textile equivalent of Salford and Manchester, before going on to sketch at Pompeii and Sorrento, still working in the same formal manner (Fig 24). Two years later, Constance began to experiment with a freer, less delineated style of

24   Constance Fielden, *Pompeii*, 1895, watercolour

painting, using longer, broader, fluid brushstrokes more quickly applied, as shown in her sketches of Margate (Fig 25), Gibraltar, Cape Roca and Jebel Musa made in 1899–1900. In the early years of the twentieth century she also tried different mediums, for example, pastel on Ingres paper (Fig 26) and different subjects, including a self-portrait (Fig 27).

It looked as though the Fieldens' troubles were almost over but on 21 December 1903, disaster struck again. An all-engulfing fire ripped through Beachamwell Hall and completely destroyed the house, leaving only the stables intact (Fig 28). The blaze had started in the library, caused by a candle being blown over by the wind but, due to the scarcity of water available to fight it, the fire soon raged out of control. Neighbours and tenants rushed to help and, amazingly, most of the valuable pictures and furniture were saved. Guests were staying at the Hall that night; theirs were the last signatures in the visitors' book for a long time. The book remained firmly closed until October 1906. In the meantime, Constance and Frances moved to Shingham House, a property on the estate just a mile away from the Hall, where they remained for the next three years. Once again, Frances was the recipient of letters of sympathy, all commiserating with her run of bad luck. Even the tenants and parishioners wrote with great sincerity of their shock and sadness at seeing such an horrific catastrophe befall the two women, while expressing their gratitude that no one had been injured and that a large proportion of the contents had been rescued from the flames.

Constance and Frances unexpectedly enjoyed their time at Shingham House. It was a traditionally pretty, neat and easy-to-run farmhouse with views across woodlands and open fields. Most importantly, proximity to Beachamwell Hall allowed the women to supervise its restoration and reconstruction, a process in which Constance was deeply involved. They decided to rebuild Beachamwell Hall as a modernised version of the original, but there was initial disagreement about the choice of architect. Unsurprisingly, this was resolved by Constance getting her

25   Constance Fielden, **North Foreland, Margate, Kent**, 1899, watercolour

26   Constance Fielden, **The Ilex Wood**, 1900,
pastel on Ingres paper

27   Constance Fielden, *Self-Portrait*, c.1905, watercolour

28   The remains of Beachamwell Hall after the fire, December 1903,
silver gelatin print

own way. Frances favoured appointing someone of her own generation and opted for a well-known, established architect, Reginald Blomfield, but Constance overruled her by insisting on engaging a younger practice to do the work. Eventually, Wimperis and Best, a firm located in Vigo Street, London, was selected. The practice was just four years old but it had already acquired a good reputation for country house building. Edmund Wimperis was ten years older than Constance, ambitious and talented, and they seemed to be very much on the same wavelength. He was eager to add to his portfolio to make sure his company appeared more modern than Reginald Blomfield's. Importantly, they could undercut the fees Blomfield commanded and, ultimately, this could have induced Frances to back her daughter's choice. The firm had also been commissioned to build Little Massingham House for a near neighbour, Mrs E. W. Birkbeck, based on the design of Bixley Hall near Norwich. Both Little Massingham House and Beachamwell Hall share some similar features: two storeys plus attics, a central pedimented hooded doorcase (Fig 29), sash windows and ridge chimney stacks.

Plans for Beachamwell Hall were drawn up and approved and, towards the end of 1906, the building was completed very much in line with the original plans but with less decorative detail than the architects had wanted. The result was a happy compromise between the beauty of a classical Queen Anne/Georgian hybrid house and the superior convenience of a modern dwelling. It represented a sharp contrast to the predominant Gothic style of the Victorian era, making the owners seem almost avant-garde. In this one rare instance, Frances and Constance overlooked historical purism in favour of comfort, and they were unabashedly in love with the Hall's mock-period look. It fulfilled all their social aspirations: it was large enough for house parties and perfect in every way for entertaining, having the necessary facilities for tennis, riding and shooting, together with outbuildings for carriages and, as was becoming increasingly common, cars. Constance and Frances had also

29 Beachamwell Hall, designed by Wimperis & Best,
illustration in *Builder* magazine, 10 November 1906

requested a painting room/studio to be designed and built on the first floor, which became a sanctuary and somewhere Constance would retreat to throughout the rest of her life. Another feature of similar importance to mother and daughter was a large, well-designed contemporary garden full of young saplings and beautiful flowers. They collaborated with the architects to plan a layout and planting scheme which promised to be stunning when fully mature and bring them great joy in the future.

In 1905, shortly before building work on the Hall had finished, Constance went abroad with friends and relatives, but without her mother. Confinement in a place that was not truly her home, constraints on her usual travel schedule and restrictions on indoor entertaining had all taken their toll and brought a longing for escape, conviviality, warmth and sunshine. Her destination was Madeira, and arriving there was like emerging into light from a long, dark shadowy existence. While there, Constance made numerous studies of heads – men, women and children in a variety of hats and poses – and her sketchbook shows a newfound delight in the combination of pencil and coloured pastels which she had tried before, but now embraced wholeheartedly in a more free-flowing style. Landscapes, interiors and gardens were her main subject focus, and she devoted a large part of one sketchbook to them (Figs 30 and 31).

Back in Norfolk, Constance was overjoyed when she and her mother moved back to the Hall. The visitors' book reopened on 4 September 1906 when guests poured in to see the house and congratulate its occupants on their achievement. Significantly, the first name to appear on its pages, and frequently thereafter, was that of Patrick Villiers Stuart (1879–1949), the man destined to become Constance's husband (Fig 32). Sometime between 1904 and 1906, they had met, developed a serious relationship and become engaged. Constance was approaching her thirtieth birthday – a milestone and, at the time, the equivalent of spinsterhood. It must have been of some relief to her and her anxious mother when Patrick proposed in 1906.

30   Constance Fielden, *In the Garden*, March 1905,
pencil and pastel

31   Constance Fielden, *The Hospital*, 1905, pencil and pastel

32   Unknown, *Portrait of Patrick Villiers Stuart*
(1879–1949), c.1906, toned silver gelatin print

In July of that year, Patrick's widowed mother, Mary Villiers Stuart, wrote to Frances from her home in Ireland to thank her for allowing Constance to marry her son. Patrick had good aristocratic credentials, but the family wasn't rich. Just as Frances would have been relieved that a candidate of good lineage, of whom she approved, had asked Constance to marry him, Mary was equally happy knowing her son had attracted a wealthy woman. One of nine siblings, Patrick's financial outlook was precarious. He knew that when his mother eventually died and her remaining chattels were divided amongst her children, each share would be relatively modest. Therefore, Constance and Patrick had struck a transactional arrangement, possibly unspoken, which suited both their aspirations, but fortunately there was genuine affection and respect on both sides. Mary Villiers Stuart praised her son's constancy and good character: 'It is more than good of you to entrust your child to him. I feel quite sure that as far as he himself is concerned you will never have cause to repent of doing this. ... your daughter has found someone who will always shield and protect her to the best of his power.'

By the late summer of 1906, Beachamwell was a happier place. A photograph taken shortly after the announcement of the engagement shows a convivial group assembled on the steps in front of the newly built Hall (Fig 33). The bride-to-be, wearing an elaborate hat (the same one as in Fig 27), is seated at the front in the centre next to Patrick. Behind her is her mother and, on the far-right outer edge of the party, one of her uncles. Constance is dressed fashionably, as if she had stepped straight from the boulevards of Belle Époque Paris. Her modish straw hat, with its layers of ruffled tulle rising high above the hat's crown, and her lace-trimmed high-necked dress, enhanced by a string of pearls, give her a distinct air of privilege and authority. There is no denying her elegance and self-assurance, but there is also a steely look at odds with the romantic apparel, one that refutes any suggestion of feminine docility. Her mother and other family members are in the background

33   Unknown, Constance Fielden with her mother and unidentified aunts and uncles, Beachamwell Hall, *c.*1906, silver gelatin print

literally, as well as metaphorically, as Constance occupies her natural place: centre stage.

Patrick had much to commend him. Educated at Charterhouse School, he was a tall, good-looking man of slim build with dark hair, piercing eyes and impeccable manners. Having grown up in Ireland at Dromana House, a beautiful residence overlooking the Blackwater River in Cappoquin, County Waterford, Patrick was at heart a country man and loved the outdoor life which, for Frances, was an essential qualification in a son-in-law. He enjoyed shooting and fishing and, crucially, once married, he took a great deal of interest in farming practices on the Beachamwell estate, recommending improvements and urging budgetary restraint. Already enlisted in the Army when he met Constance, Patrick was for a short time aide-de-camp to the Governor of Madras, Sir Arthur Lawley, before going on to have a distinguished military career with the 2nd Battalion Royal Fusiliers in India and later, during the First World War, in Salonica.

The wedding took place at St Paul's Church, Wilton Place, Knightsbridge, on 26 February 1908. Numerous guests gathered on what was a particularly cold but sunny day in central London, to celebrate the ceremony and to feast afterwards at the opulent Alexandra Hotel.[3] Well-wishers included prominent families from Lancashire, Norfolk and Ireland, personal friends and relatives, and many tenants from the Dromana and Beachamwell estates. This was a minor society event, but nevertheless a fashionable and expensive one which featured in the press coverage of the day. Constance, attended by four bridesmaids, was dressed in white chiffon, 'with a wreath of satin flowers round the bodice, a broad empire sash of satin crossed at the back through an old paste buckle and falling to the hem of the train'. She wore 'a tulle veil with a coronet of orange and myrtle blossoms, and carried a bouquet of white exotics'. The bridesmaids, among them Constance's best friend, watercolourist and diarist Edith Upcher, all wore 'artistic' outfits in the 'Romany Style' made of pale grey chiffon, decorated with oxidised silver embroidery and sprays of silver flowers. Their statement hats were created from grey net, trimmed with vieux rose velvet and carnations. Uniformed officers of the Royal Fusiliers lined the aisle as Patrick and his best man, the Honourable Claud Chichester, also resplendent in their red and gold-trimmed uniforms, strode towards the waiting bride, adding a glamorous military swagger to the scene.

Constance and Patrick Villiers Stuart spent their honeymoon on the Riviera, which had been a favourite destination of the Fielden family for more than thirty years. Cannes, Antibes, Nice and Menton in France and Bodighera in Italy were even more fashionable in the early twentieth-century than they had been when Frances Fielden was a regular visitor in the 1870s and 1880s. In addition to royalty, aristocracy and immensely wealthy Americans, the area had become synonymous with artists and writers who sought not just the intensity of its light, natural beauty and perfect climate, but also the lavish parties, grand hotels and tempting casinos. From late autumn to early spring, celebrities flocked there, including Pablo Picasso, Henri Matisse, Edith Wharton, Somerset Maugham, Winston Churchill, Isadora Duncan, Pierre-Auguste Renoir, John Pierpont Morgan, Beatrice de Rothschild, Anna Pavlova and many more. For a February honeymoon, it was considered the *ne plus ultra* of resorts, and Constance and Patrick spent the rest of the winter there, finally heading home to England in late April.

The newlyweds immediately settled down to a comfortable married life at Beachamwell Hall, expending their energy on socialising and leisure pursuits. Although life was extremely pleasant, for someone as ambitious and restless as Constance, it wasn't enough – she wanted much more action. Fortunately for her, this came at the beginning of 1910, when she learned that she was pregnant, and that Patrick was being posted to India. India! The mere mention of it excited Constance far more than her pregnancy. Thanks to her husband's career, the posting was a chance for her to go somewhere she had never been before, explore the unknown and experience a whiff of danger. She needed to rekindle that sense of adventure which had first been ignited in her as a child in Australia. The thought of travelling thrilled her, but first she had to have her baby, which had become almost an inconvenience once India had come into the frame.

Constance regarded pregnancy as a requirement of convention that had to be endured rather than enjoyed, and she was delighted when it was over. A healthy daughter, Patricia Mary Villiers Stuart, was born on 28 September 1910. She was to be Constance and Patrick's only child. They jointly agreed that the baby should not accompany them to India but be left in the care of a nursery nurse and Grandmother Frances at Beachamwell. Many parents whose colonial work required them to go to India found the choice of whether or not to leave their children behind in England an almost impossible one, but it was very common to do so, and for worthy reasons: to protect them from tropical diseases, adverse reactions to the climate and the rigours of the journey.

Constance and Patricia spent only a short time together. There is only one known photograph of mother and newborn baby, taken at the Baker Street studio of Rita Martin and now faded almost to invisibility. The selection of one of London's most fashionable photographers was unsurprising; Rita Martin was a pioneer of the craft, specialising in romantic, hand-tinted images of actresses, society women and children. The secret of her great appeal was in the use of flattering, soft lighting to portray her sitters as ethereal, angelic, blemish-free visions of feminine perfection, which aligned exactly with the image Constance wished to project.

In early January 1911, shortly before leaving for India, Constance painted a small unidentified interior scene of a sitting room either at Beachamwell Hall or the Villiers Stuarts' London flat at 1 Montague Mansions, Portman Square (Fig 34), perhaps as a memento in a rare

34   Constance Villiers Stuart, *Interior*, January 1911,
watercolour

moment of nostalgia, or as a reminder of how her life had changed from the bleak period of the 1890s to her present good fortune. She also searched bookshops in London and Norwich for a guide to the Mughal gardens of India but found nothing on the subject. Characteristically, Constance said she might write one herself. With this idea percolating in her mind and the prospect of exploration ahead, she and Patrick said goodbye to Frances and Patricia and set sail for Bombay (Mumbai) aboard the SS *Castalia* on 12 January. They wouldn't return to England for two and a half years.

CHAPTER FOUR

An Indian Interlude

The passage from Liverpool to Bombay aboard SS *Castalia* was smooth and calm, almost balmy for the time of year. Constance and Patrick had hours of uninterrupted free time to fill. Between meals and lounging on deck, their days were spent playing cards and ship's billiards, swimming, dancing and reading (Figs 35 and 36). The crossing also allowed the idea of writing a book about Indian gardens to crystallise in Constance's mind, and she was encouraged by Patrick's enthusiasm for her project. Besides being a soldier, he was a keen gardener and amateur historian and relished the possibility of rooting around abandoned pleasure grounds and ancient monuments.[4] After arriving at Bombay in early February, the couple took a train from Victoria Terminus (now Chhatrapati Shivaji Terminus) and travelled 600 miles northwest to Jubbulpore (Jabalpur). They passed through the gorges, craggy ravines, thick tropical forests and grasslands of the Central Provinces of the British Raj (now Madhya Pradesh). Their impression of the region was that of a strange, rugged, quite sinister landscape. Being the cold season; the foliage was still lush and full of vines and creepers harbouring snakes, fruit bats, beautiful butterflies and dazzling flocks of multicoloured birds. Swathes of wildflowers, thickets of bamboo and tall, dense ferns hid an exciting range of wildlife: tigers, panthers, flying squirrels, monkeys, crocodiles and deer. For the new arrivals, it was all very interesting, but also slightly unsettling and unhealthy.

35   Constance Villiers Stuart, **Ship Billiards**, January 1911, pencil

36   Constance Villiers Stuart, **"Bridge" on SS Castalia**, Jan 1911, pencil

Such unfamiliar and unpredictable countryside contrasted spectacularly with the symmetrical precision of neatly uniformed soldiers regularly parading past the Villiers Stuarts' home in Jubbulpore's cantonment zone. In 1911, this was a safe haven; Jubbulpore was a modern city with wide, regularly spaced streets, well laid out and tailored to British tastes. Since 1817, it had been a strategic military headquarters and, as a result, had become an important railway hub linking the Great Indian Peninsula and the East Indian systems. A small stream divided the barracks and the European sector from the native quarter. The barracks sprawled over several miles and linked extensive training grounds and administrative buildings to a residential zone made up of spacious bungalows set in large, well-tended gardens. There were other facilities close by which, at the time, were considered essential for civilised colonial living, including Christ Church Cathedral (est. 1844), the Nerbudda (Narmada) Club (est. 1889), a parade of shops selling English products, several agencies for hiring domestic staff, and attractive parks in which to stroll. Before the Villiers Stuarts could move into their own home, they spent some time at Jackson's Hotel (Fig 37), then a grand and impressive building – now a ruin (Fig 38) – which welcomed and refreshed expatriates from Britain. Constance made a pencil drawing of its porte-cochère in her sketchbook – a tiny personal memento of her arrival in Jubbulpore during the hotel's heyday (Fig 39).

Although the couple remained at the cantonment for lengthy periods, Jubbulpore served mainly as a base from which they travelled to other parts of India. Patrick moved around to other army outposts, mostly in Delhi, Bhopal and Lahore, and Constance went to the Punjab, Uttar Pradesh, Rajasthan and Kashmir to research the history of Mughal gardens. Her growing interest in Indian culture brought with it a chance for Constance not only to establish herself as more than just an appendage to her military husband, but also to gain the respect and confidence of the Indians with whom she interacted. Everything she

37   Unknown, the original Jackson's Hotel, Jubbulpore (Jabalpur),
late nineteenth century, albumen print

38   Author, Jackson's Hotel today, Jubbulpore (Jabalpur), 2019, digital print

39   Constance Villiers Stuart, *Jackson's Hotel, Jubbulpore*, 1911, pencil

achieved on her initial visit to India gave her value there, as well as in Britain, Europe and the USA, for the rest of her life. But before she began to explore other parts of India beyond Jubbulpore, Constance sought to understand better the design aspects of a Mughal garden in a practical way, by creating an Indian *bagh*[5] of her own.

The Villiers Stuarts' bungalow, near Jubbulpore's Civil Lines Road, was well appointed and visible from the street, with about two acres of land around it, which Constance described as 'a burnt-out field'. During the spring of 1911 she began working with her *malis*[6] to plan the layout. She had a distinct vision of what she wanted and, having already gleaned enough knowledge of Indian gardens to know that water features were crucial to their design, her first task was to install a fountain. She planted native flowers around the borders of the garden – irises, roses, marigolds (perfect for repelling mosquitoes), dahlias, carnations, chrysanthemums and jasmine – then she added flowering fruit trees and other indigenous saplings, as well as raised walkways to suggest greater Mughal authenticity. There was even a permanent resident cobra, a propitious symbol, living under one of the mango trees and fed daily with an offering of milk.

Through such efforts, Constance expressed respect for Indian traditions and emphasised her resistance to English horticultural influences. She was immensely proud of her Jubbulpore garden and frequently cited it in her later years, for example, in her application to the Institute of Landscape Architects (ILA) in 1942, when she included it in her list of design projects under the simple title of 'Irrigated Water-Garden'. A photograph taken in the summer of 1911 (Fig 40) shows Constance seated by the fountain surrounded by flowers. Even today, the basic plan of her original garden remains intact.

Constance's opinion of the planting and design of Jubbulpore's public spaces was largely negative; she was particularly critical of King's Gardens (Tagore Gardens) and its environs. She made general remarks about

40   Unknown, Constance Villiers Stuart in her garden, Jubbulpore, 1911,
albumen print

the awfulness of British-designed Indian parks, but Tagore Gardens, which was close to her home, matched all her criteria for offensiveness, the chief problems being '... bare acres of unhappy-looking grass, ... ugly bandstands, hideous iron railings, and forlorn European statues; ... wide, objectless roads, scattered flower-beds, and solitary trees, and worst of all in a hot country, their lack of fountains and running water'.

Despite so many apparently risible features, the park today is a much loved and frequented place. It now has fountains and running water, so perhaps Constance's harsh words eventually filtered through to future city planners and designers.

Overall, Constance objected to the way in which typical Indian garden craft, based on religious symbolism, was being altered or completely destroyed:

> Wherever English influence has been strong, as in British
> India and the so-called "progressive" native states, ... Indian
> gardens have been the first to go. ... In place of the stately
> water-ways and avenues, the pergolas and gay parterres,
> the perfumed dusk of the Hindu pleasure-grounds, and the
> sunshine brilliance of the Mughal baghs, the incongruities of
> the Anglo-Indian landscape gardener reign supreme.

With the fervency of a conservationist, Constance began mounting a one-woman campaign for the preservation, restoration and continued use of Indian heritage sites, and for new garden designs to respect the past. She wanted British architects and planners to replicate historic Indian layouts and planting rather than imposing a purely English vision wherever they went. What she saw during those first few months in Jubbulpore inspired Constance to rethink what might be possible for new landscape garden projects in India. One instance she witnessed in Jubbulpore set her on a course which would eventually see her lobbying the architects Edwin Lutyens and Herbert Baker and their clients, the

Viceroy of India and his wife, Lord and Lady Hardinge, to modify the gardens of Viceroy's House (Rashtrapati Bhavan) in New Delhi.

One of her neighbours in Jubbulpore, whom she described as 'a wealthy merchant prince of the Jain caste', was rebuilding an Anglo-Indian bungalow and had decided to transform the grass compound around it into a garden. The prince removed the curved drive leading to the front door and replaced it with a straight one, which extended at the back of the house; he then added straight horizontal paths at both sides of the building, so that all four lines ran in the cardinal directions like the four waterways (Charbagh) design of Mughal gardens. Over the ensuing weeks more traditional features appeared: a purdah (secluded) garden for the women of the family in one of the quadrangles, and several white marble shrines under a line of trees. Two fountains with large basins encircled by Mughal-style parterres graced either side of the front entrance, and an elegant terrace enhanced by decorative *chabutras*[7] added further charm to the design scheme. In a flamboyant gesture, the prince laid a special round 'English' lawn on which he displayed a bust of King Emperor George V; he then augmented the entire scene by introducing some tame fawns to graze on the beautifully mown grass. The mélange of East and West did not appeal to everyone; it was widely described as 'quaint, queer, inexplicable and frankly hideous'. Yet Constance said the result was '… the most interesting experiment in the making of a modern Indian garden I have seen'.

After witnessing the development of the Jain prince's garden, Constance was sure that she had discovered something significant: the necessity of engaging Indian advisors, artists and craftsmen to work on British architectural and landscape design projects in India in order to ensure a respectful cross-cultural exchange of ideas. Originally, before she settled on Mughal gardens as her chosen subject, Constance had had a vague plan of writing about modern Indian gardens, but when she arrived in India she could not find interesting contemporary examples, nor any being planned, apart from the one at Viceroy's House in New Delhi. The few smaller-scale new gardens she did see were those by British expatriates who recreated English models and who, in her opinion, took a great interest in their gardens in India only because they were incentivised by the rapid growth and novelty of native flowers and trees, and the readily available cheap labour.

Consequently, Constance decided definitively to focus on historic Indian gardens which, so far as she knew, had not been written about before, and certainly not from a female perspective. Her hunch was confirmed by a trivial incident highlighting the need for more knowledge about the country's historic gardens. While travelling on a train across northern India, Constance struck up a conversation with another British passenger whose wide knowledge of India's history impressed her. When she glanced out of the window she saw 'a blurred, but entrancing vision of red enclosing walls, high tiled gateways, and slender marble minarets, rising through the densely clustering palms and forest trees of a great garden'. She asked the stranger what it was. He did not know; instead, he just shrugged and dismissed it as 'another of those old Mughal baghs'.

Constance was always convinced that her ideas were good ones, but she still needed to be better informed in order to convert others to her cause. Her solution was to visit as many historic sites as she could physically manage, research the subject thoroughly and engage the support of well-known connoisseurs. She was extremely diligent in her quest for assistance, consulting many, and sometimes forming friendships with, leading contemporary experts on India. Among them were the archaeologist, Sir Aurel Stein; the art historian and educationalist, E. B. Havell; the architectural historian, James Fergusson; the polymath and arts administrator, Sir George Birdwood; and John Begg, the Head of Architecture at Edinburgh College of Art. She read their books and corresponded with them; afterwards she studied Indian miniatures and absorbed the memoirs of the first Emperor and founder of the Mughal

Dynasty, Zahīr-ud-Dīn Muhammad Babur (1483–1530), whose love of gardens was legendary. Firsthand experience was vital, so she decided to make objective photographic records of Mughal sites for her book, then add some of her own colourful and attractive watercolour drawings to personalise it. She believed her expertise would then position her favourably to advise on garden design in India and, for an amateur, she set her sights high, aiming to get involved with the planning and execution of Viceroy's House and its garden.

In a nod to her northern ancestors' thirst for innovation and experimentation (but without any of their profit motive), Constance described her venture as an attempt to 'break fresh ground'. Like many women of her time, she longed to achieve something noteworthy of her own volition, to have her voice heard and be taken seriously. Therefore, she spent most of the next eighteen months conducting research in Delhi, Agra, Jaipur, Udaipur, Lahore, Islamabad and Srinagar, with intervals back in Jubbulpore. She packed a camera, notebooks, sketchpads, watercolours and paintbrushes, painting clothes and several suitcases of smart outfits so that she could be suitably dressed for encounters with Indian nobility. Sometimes Patrick joined her and at other times she travelled alone, hiring servants en route and relying on her precious clutch of introductions from influential friends and acquaintances to smooth her path. By enlisting the help of friends like HH the Maji Sahiba of Bharatpur, HH Princess Bamba Duleep Singh and HH the Begam of Bhopal, she was assured of hospitality in the highest Indian circles throughout her expedition.

LAHORE AND KASHMIR

Constance made several trips to Kashmir in 1911 and 1912, beginning with a two-month trek spanning September to October 1911. She went via Lahore to see the famous Shalimar Gardens (Shalimar Bagh), one of the most perfect, albeit partially desecrated, examples of a Mughal garden, laid out to represent the Koranic ideal of a heavenly garden 'underneath which rivers will flow' and where believers would reside 'in perpetual abode'. One of Shalimar's distinguishing and well-preserved features was the use of patterned brickwork for the pathways between rows of fountains. These were quite unlike those of Delhi and Agra and, as Constance's painting of the entrance to the Bagh shows (Fig 41), more beautiful. When she painted Shalimar, the gardens were abundant and lovely, but still not above provoking her criticism:

> At the Lahore Shalimar, the mistake has recently been made
> of trying to grow … flowers in the shallow canals, which
> only results in making the water muddy, and confusing the
> effect of the range of little fountains. On the other hand, if
> grown round the central chabutra of the large tank the lotus
> would look very well, for the plants themselves cannot be
> seen to advantage unless they are given plenty of space and
> deep water.

Constance always had ideas of how to upgrade what she saw. She had sympathy, respect and a liking for Indian culture, but it came from the perspective of knowing what was best for India and how things might be improved by the ruling power. Her views matched those of the era in which she lived, romanticising the country and its people and feeling morally obliged, in a racially superior way, 'to do something' to help it realise its potential. Consequently, she identified with, and felt a strong affinity for, the Mughal rulers who had aggressively transformed Indian art and architecture. From her perspective, Indians should be encouraged to employ their traditional skills for architectural and landscape design projects, but under British direction and in line with colonial proclivities.

Constance was interested in the intangible qualities of Shalimar Gardens, how that inside-outside life might once have been lived by

41   Constance Villiers Stuart, **The Old Entrance,
Shalimar Bagh, Lahore**, 1911, an original painting (now lost)
from which Plate XXII, *Gardens of the Great Mughals*
(Adam & Charles Black, 1913) was reproduced

women in the *zenana*, or by the emperors holding audiences in private or public spaces (Diwan-e-Khas and Diwan-e-Aam respectively), or by the courtiers who served them. Referencing carpets and Mughal paintings, she recalled the music that might have been played and the instruments that would have been used to play it; the poems that would have been read; the furniture, the clothes and accessories; the splash of fountains, the beauty of flowers and fruits along the pathways, and all the scents that would have filled the air. When she left Lahore, she wrote of Shalimar: 'As melancholy, ghost-haunted as it is, still one leaves it with regret – this old garden-palace full of echoes.' As she scribbled her notes and sketched impressions in watercolour, Constance absorbed the vapours of the past impinging on the present; she sensed the actions and voices of former generations resonating in her mind and she tried her best to capture them for a contemporary audience.

Shahdara, on the banks of the Ravi River about five miles north of Lahore, was once the entry point of that city from Kabul and Kashmir. It is now a poor, dusty village, but from the early sixteenth century it was a site for royal tombs. Emperor Jahangir was buried at Shahdara in the Dilkusha Bagh, a very large garden laid out by his wife, Nur Jahan, and it was here that Constance made a painting, now lost,[8] of the view through the great arched doorway leading to a courtyard (Fig 42) She praised the climbing plants, the fountains and the cypress trees, but bemoaned the general sparsity of the borders around the lawns. Longing for an almost imaginary past where every garden was richly planted and flowering brightly, where fountains played incessantly, and attractive people walked languidly within the grounds, Constance writes wistfully of the degeneration and demise of the Mughal garden – but Shahdara has survived intact, albeit run-down, to the present day and remains a pleasant public space where people enjoy picnicking and passing their leisure time. Constance's zeal for preserving ancient Mughal sites was not common among her compatriots nor many Indians at that time, and

42   Constance Villiers Stuart, **Shah-Dara**, 1911, an original painting
(now lost) from which Plate XIX, *Gardens of the Great Mughals*
was reproduced

it was not until the late twentieth century that masterplans were drawn up to manage, protect and upgrade this particular heritage site. Work there continues to this day.

Leaving the Punjab from Rawalpindi, the Villiers Stuarts travelled together towards Kashmir, a place then especially beloved of the British, glorified as the fabled land of Lalla Rookh, the Vale of Paradise and, for Constance, the Jewel of the Mughal Empire. They followed the southern route to Srinagar, visiting Anantnag and the nearby archaeological site of the Sun Temple at Martand, then spending some time at the gardens of Verinag and Achabal before exploring parts of the Liddar Valley. From there, they continued to Avantipur and on to Srinagar. In October, they went north to visit Sopore and the lakes at Manasbal and Wular, the latter the largest lake in Kashmir.

Although past their seasonal peak of beauty, the Kashmiri lakes in autumn were still spectacular, encircled by yellowing willows, swaying poplars and fruit trees heavily laden with apples, walnuts and hazelnuts. The Mughal *baghs* dotted around the springs and lakes were not too crowded and the weather was cooler, which made it a good time to discover the pleasures of Kashmir. In the background, rose the beautiful Pir Panjal mountains. They were useful, too, playing an essential role in replenishing the gardens by feeding the streams and rivers during the annual spring melt. From March to May water rushed through ravines and fell to the valley floor where it was diverted to the canals, fountains and tanks of the Mughal palaces.

In early autumn, when blue skies and white clouds reflected in the lakes, and greenery was still abundant, scents of dust and flowers going to seed hinted at the change of season. In a sudden riot of colour, like the final flicker of a guttering candle, zinnias, marigolds, petunias and dahlias, and even melons and pumpkins, produced a grand finale. During the day, the sun was hot, but not enough to prevent sketching from a shady spot; it was only during the evenings and nights that the chill of approaching winter was discernible. Naturally, Constance and Patrick fell in love with Kashmir; it was impossible not to. As much as they were there for a purpose, they also loved fishing, hunting, socialising and adventure, all the things which had given Kashmir a reputation as one of the great playgrounds of Asia. For artists, it was irresistible: the alpine landscape together with relics of antiquity – the temples, mosques, mausoleums, gardens and grottoes – provided so much to admire and record.

At various intervals along the route, Constance stopped to sketch the scenery (Figs 43, 44, 45, 46 and 47). It was not easy to do justice to the vistas in front of her, and she was certainly not alone in a problem many previous writers, poets and artists had wrestled with. Maud Diver, a British writer of romantic fiction, best described the beauty of Kashmir as neither India nor not-India, but a sublime impersonal world of its own somewhere 'between heaven and earth'. Undaunted by forerunners, Constance made pencil sketches of the ruins at Martand, capturing their awe-inspiring size and monumentality (Fig 48). At nearby Achabal (Achabal), she painted a watercolour sketch of the poolside pavilion surrounded by wilting trees and backed by snow-capped mountains (Fig 49), which she later modified for publication (Fig 50). *Autumn at Achibal* (Plate XXIX, *Gardens of the Great Mughals*), shows how Constance concealed the mountains with heavy clouds and removed two poplar trees, possibly in an attempt to create a more autumnal atmosphere. Achabal, as it is shown here, is a small, terraced garden, with freezing water gushing from a spring and cascading like a sheet over a waterfall (Figs 51 and 52). Constance thought it an ideal site and wrote 'If I were asked where the most perfect modern garden on a medium scale could be devised, I should answer without hesitation "Achibal".' Just over a decade later, the writer and traveller Aldous Huxley thought the trees and waters of Achabal the loveliest of all the Kashmiri gardens, although, unlike Constance, he attributed its beauty more to nature than its architecture. She thought neither more important than the other, but

43   Constance Villiers Stuart, *On the road to Avantipur*, 1911,
watercolour sketch

44   Constance Villiers Stuart, *On the road to Avantipur*, 1911,
watercolour sketch

45   Constance Villiers Stuart, **On the road to Avantipur**, 1911,
watercolour sketch

46   Constance Villiers Stuart, **On the road to Avantipur**, 1911,
watercolour sketch

47   Constance Villiers Stuart, **On the road to Avantipur**, 1911,
watercolour sketch

48   Constance Villiers Stuart, **North Entrance, Martand**, 1911, pencil sketch

49   Constance Villiers Stuart, **Achibal**, 1911, watercolour sketch

50   Plate XXIX, taken from the above sketch for *Gardens of the Great
Mughals* (Adam & Charles Black, 1913)

51 Constance Villiers Stuart, **The Great Waterfall**, September 1911, pencil sketch, Achibal Bagh

52 Constance Villiers Stuart, **The Great Waterfall**, Plate XXVIII, in *Gardens of the Great Mughals*, from original watercolour, Achibal Bagh

that perfect interdependence and harmony between the garden and its contained house created the best aesthetic experience. Balance between the two elements superseded individual merits, each enhancing the best qualities of the other.

Dal Lake ('The Lake of Flowers') in Srinagar was the beating heart of Constance's Kashmiri inquiry. The entire lake was (and remains to this day) surrounded by Mughal gardens great and small, the most important of which are Shalimar Bagh and Nishat Bagh. The rapturous poetry of Thomas Moore, in his ode to Lalla Rookh, the fictional daughter of Mughal emperor Aurangzeb, had set British expectations high for an encounter with Lake Dal:

> 'Who in moonlight and music this sweetly may glide
> O'er the lake of Cashmere with that One by his side!
> If woman can make the worst wilderness dear,
> Think, think what a heaven she must make of Cashmere.'

However, by 1911 romance had been replaced by commerce; Constance might have been disappointed to find the lake covered in thick beds of reeds and bulrushes, on which sat assorted floating gardens surrounded by frantic activity, with people coming and going, buying and selling, loading and unloading. She and Patrick hired boatmen to ferry them to the lakeside gardens, but it was not always an enjoyable experience. Artificial lanes had to be cut though the vegetation so that boats could get across the lake, and these were crowded with traders and groups of pleasure seekers. It was also not the best time to see the flowers for which the region was famed, although, within the lakeside *baghs*, the system of irrigation allowed for a bright display of autumnal blooms.

The Villiers Stuarts completed their first expedition to Kashmir at the end of October, but they vowed to return the following spring when the region's flowers would be reaching the height of their beauty. Whilst the tour had not been a very long one, it had been enough to make

Constance excited about the wealth of Kashmiri experiences yet to be had. Back in Jubbulpore, they prepared to go to Agra in November and, from there, to Delhi in December, where Patrick had been summoned for a week of formal duties. The 2nd Battalion Royal Fusiliers would be taking part in the much-anticipated Delhi Durbar.

AGRA

For Constance, Agra would be a major highlight of her life. Of all the great Mughal buildings in India, the Taj Mahal[9] is considered the finest. As a subject which has been tackled successfully many times in the past, it is hard for any artist or writer to put a new spin on such a famous monument. Constance acknowledged the impediment, saying that her own impressions might be redundant were it not that most previous attempts to capture the beauty and grandeur of this garden-tomb concentrated solely on the building, rather than its garden. She, however, purposely went to record the whole design of the building and its integrated garden. Taking a bold vantage point, facing the Taj but from a distance, Constance ensured the structure, central water feature and the avenue of cypresses were represented equally (Fig 53). Seeing and recording this site was a singular artistic experience, and one which stood out forever in her memory. On publication, the *Aberdeen Journal* described this particular painting, entitled *The Gates were as of Pearl*, as 'entrancing' and 'full of charm'.

She recalled how cold it was on the misty November morning when she first set eyes on the Taj shortly after dawn, and also how annoyed the doorkeeper had been when she shook him awake to ask for the gates to be opened early so that she could paint in peace. He acquiesced, and Constance found herself totally alone in the grounds – a rare event in itself – facing an eerie, empty, grey and ghostly vision; the Taj 'loomed' out of the mist, 'cheerless' against the sky, but as the sun rose it seemed to her that a miracle had been revealed. She had a momentary revelation

53   Constance Villiers Stuart, **The Gates were as of Pearl**, 1911, watercolour,
private collection

of being present in the seventeenth century, imagining how the design had been conceived, planned and realised, then taken on a life of its own as a world-renowned monument to femininity. The 'effeminacy' of the Taj Mahal had been criticised in the nineteenth century by those who thought it too pretty and dainty, but Constance agreed with the eminent scholar E. B. Havell who thought such a description was the highest tribute the critics could pay to the genius of the builders and the intentions of the designers.

Although Constance had been physically present in front of the Taj Mahal and painted what she saw, her final watercolour is a direct copy of a lantern slide (Fig 54). She used photography as an *aide-memoire* for this and many other buildings which were ultimately included in *Gardens of the Great Mughals*, such as Sikhandrah (Sikandra), just outside Agra, and Nishat Bagh in Kashmir. Constance's interest in photography was not just to jog her memory when she returned to her studio to finish her paintings; she amassed a large collection of slides in India to illustrate the public lectures she was planning to give when she was back in Britain, and others were eventually used for articles she wrote for various magazines after her book had been published.

Constance painted several views of the Taj Mahal at different times of day to capture the changes of light, as in *Evening in the Garden of the Taj* (Fig 55), and *Agra from the Taj* (Fig 56), where she focused on the buildings at sunset, making preliminary sketches which emphasised the reddening sky (Fig 57). This site was the sole focus of her artistic efforts while she was in Agra, and although she wrote at length about others including Ram Bagh, the oldest Mughal garden in India, the architecture at nearby Fatehpur Sikri and Akbar's Tomb at Sikandra, there are no drawings or paintings of them, which indicates that garden research in and around Agra was done in a hurry.

In her book Constance made a strong and prescient case for the conservation of the Garden of the Tomb of I'timad-ud-Daulah[10] on the

54   Unknown, *The Taj Mahal*, c.1911, hand-coloured glass
lantern slide, from Constance Villiers Stuart's personal collection of
photographs

55   Constance Villiers Stuart, **An Evening in the Garden of the Taj**,
1911, watercolour from which Plate V, *Gardens of the Great Mughals* was
reproduced, private collection

56   Constance Villiers Stuart, **Agra from the Taj**, 1911, watercolour
from which Plate XII, *Gardens of the Great Mughals* was reproduced,
private collection

57   Constance Villiers Stuart, watercolour sketch for **Agra from the Taj**, 1911

eastern bank of the Yamuna River at Agra. Sometimes called 'baby Taj', the building was created by Empress Nur Jahan in 1622 in the memory of her Persian parents and is exquisitely embellished with inlaid stones and tiles – owing much to the culture of their forefathers. By the time Constance made a tour of inspection in 1911, the garden had fallen into neglect. Once again, she recited her oft-repeated litany of failings: empty water channels looking 'meaningless and forlorn', bare mown grass plots, an absence of fruit trees and flowers, and a lack of 'glittering fountain spray'. The garden's relative smallness made it, according to Constance, a realistic prospect for repair and the recovery of its former glory, when the 'flash and sparkle of water' soothed the soul and the rose-bushes 'dropped their petals in tribute' to the deceased.

The rest of the twentieth century wreaked further damage on the site through urban growth, climate change, traffic congestion and pollution, but a five-year project completed in 2019 restored the gardens to their original form and reactivated the water features. Over a hundred years since she wrote her plea to save the garden, Constance's wish was fulfilled through the World Monument Fund, in partnership with the Archaeological Survey of India. Now, as she envisaged, visitors in the midst of a congested city can experience the four requisite Mughal elements of shade, water, fruit and fragrance and enjoy walking in cleaner air.

DELHI

The Delhi Durbar of 1911 (7–16 December) was an enormous public spectacle of pageantry and military might, calculated to cement British authority in India and improve Anglo-Indian relations in the face of growing nationalism. King George V's lavish and popular ascension to the throne in Britain earlier in the year[11] provided the perfect reason for a repeat performance of beauty, drama and pomp in Delhi to show the world the extent of British power. There were other reasons too: the King intended to use the solemnity of the occasion to announce that the capital city was going to transfer from Calcutta to Delhi, something that had been kept secret to all but six people in the months preceding the Durbar; additionally, King George and Queen Mary were to be crowned Emperor and Empress of India in front of the country's nobility, the princes, nawabs and maharajas through whom Britain wielded its power and control. Each one would be presented individually to their majesties and pay obeisance to them. Within the impressive gathering of male potentates there would be one lone woman, the Begum of Bhopal, who was one of Constance's good friends. It promised to be an unforgettable occasion, one where Constance anticipated making herself known to people of influence.

Such a major historical event had required meticulous planning and a lot of money, approximately £120 million. The site chosen for this extravaganza was a park near Burari Road, not far from Nirankari Sarovar in north Delhi, known as Coronation Park. A vast tented city was erected in just four months and took the form of a gigantic amphitheatre comprising a post office, a railway station with ten platforms, two polo grounds and three small hospitals. In addition, there were abundant gardens, a small farm, silk-lined tents with several rooms for the royal and vice-regal entourages, and elaborate *shamianas*[12] for the maharajas. The King's camp alone occupied eighty-five acres, replete with new roads, lawns[13] and red roses imported from England. On Durbar Day, 12 December, crowds of guests gathered together with an immense phalanx of military personnel, making a total of some 250,000 people.

At the centre of the amphitheatre were the royal canopy and throne, where the King and Queen sat like deities, wearing full coronation robes and regalia in which they sweltered despite it being winter in India. Their majesties' regal comportment and rich accoutrements were almost invisible to a viewer seated at the outer rim of the amphitheatre, from where they would have appeared like distant pinpricks. Fortunately,

Patrick and Constance held reserved seats in a prime position – the second row from the front – from where they witnessed the entire proceedings with an unimpeded view.

Constance loved ceremonial occasions not only for reasons of social advancement but also because she was genuinely interested in innovation; she marvelled at the newly installed electricity, writing:

> One of the most pleasing features from an artistic point
> of view was the really fine use made of electricity for
> illuminations on a large scale. This was particularly
> noticeable in the Indian camps, some belonging to the
> greater princes, glowing each night with fairy-like festoons,
> beautiful in colour and design; for once, Western innovation
> well applied, helping to carry out a scheme of Eastern art.

Constance's interest in the decorative features of the Delhi Durbar reflected her view that the British could not, and should not, ignore Indian ideals in any of their ceremonial or architectural undertakings. Some fellow Britons felt that pandering to these ideals was a sign of weakness and could be interpreted as a loosening of Britain's grip on maintaining order. Constance, on the other hand, considered that showing respect for India's heritage was a sign of British confidence in its position. She, unlike many visitors, recognised the symbolism of the gold-embroidered umbrella held aloft over the head of King George V. It signified a sheltering sacred tree, and when the King vacated his throne leaving the umbrella unattended, Constance saw crowds of Indians kneeling in prayer before it. Another feature she greatly admired was the carved wooden railings beside the gateway to the Maharaja of Kashmir's camp which she described as the most beautiful and satisfactory examples of modern Indian craftsmanship.

The Delhi Durbar was a successful pageant of praise for the King Emperor and for Britain, but it was also an excuse for a week-long party.

There were brass bands playing throughout the day, cricket and polo matches, point-to-point races, lunches, receptions and dinners. On one of these occasions, Patrick and Constance were introduced to the Viceroy and Governor-General of India, Lord Hardinge, and his wife, the Vicereine of India, Lady Hardinge. Constance, with her inimitable gift for polite opportunism, seized the moment to display her awareness of plans for the new Viceroy's House and grounds in New Delhi and to impress them with her newly acquired knowledge of Kashmiri gardens. The meeting was a great success and it motivated Constance, for she now had a direct connection to Lord Hardinge and could, forthwith, contact him whenever she wanted to give advice – whether he wanted it or not.

Constance saw all the famous sites while she was in Delhi: the market at Chandni Chowk, Humayum's garden-tomb, Qutab Minar, Purana Qila, Jama Masjid, Safdarjung Tomb and Shalimar Bagh, but painted just one of them, the Diwan-i-Khas or Hall of Private Audience (Fig 58) at the Red Fort.[14] In the nineteenth century, this palace-fortress was inhabited by Bahadur Shah Zafar, the last Mughal Emperor, until he was exiled to Rangoon, Burma (now Yangon, Myanmar) by the British in 1858 for the part he had played in the 1857 Rebellion. Constance's painting depicts the white marble single-storey building which was once inlaid with coloured gemstones in floral designs, most of which had been plundered by the time of her visit. The gardens at the fort had been completely renovated for the Durbar so that where previously there had been a wilderness, there were now sparkling fountains, water runnels, shrubberies, flower beds and manicured lawns. In Constance's composition, she gives equal importance to the garden and the building with a great splash of red flowers in the foreground. When the painting was published in *Gardens of the Great Mughals*, she used it to emphasise the decline and tragic end of the Mughal Empire and the 'greatest of the arts and crafts it fostered'.

58   Constance Villiers Stuart, **The Diwan-i-Khas**,
Plate XVII in *Gardens of the Great Mughals*, 1913,
from the original watercolour, Delhi

CHAPTER FIVE

Preparation and Publication

What a difference a few months made, after the winter of 1911 had made way for the spring of 1912. Constance was in a buoyant mood as she began her second excursion to Kashmir in April, rhapsodising about the abundance of colourful flowers covering the mountain foothills, confident of the future success of her book and eager to finish her research and cement the relationships she had made at the Delhi Durbar. Kashmir was inspiring, fresh and exciting, and the scenery even more ravishing than the previous autumn. Now, when the Mughal gardens were aglow with yellow and purple crocuses, daisies, heartsease, carmine-striped tulips, almond blossom, yellow mustard flowers and many varieties of iris, Constance set herself the specific task of making an in-depth study of the two influential lakeside gardens, Shalimar Bagh ('Abode of Love') and Nishat Bagh ('Garden of Delights'). She settled in for a six-month stint in and around Srinagar and returned only infrequently to Jabalpur during 1912, seeing Patrick intermittently when he came to Kashmir to join her on painting expeditions during which he also made his own sketches in pencil and watercolour. Later in 1912, Constance visited other towns and cities in northern India including Pinjore in Haryana, and the British summer capital, Shimla, in Himachal Pradesh.

It is uncertain where Constance lived during her extended stay in Kashmir. Some sketches suggest she might have spent time at Nedou's, a pair of fashionable European hotels at Srinagar and Gulmarg. It is certainly hard to imagine her living, like many tourists, on a houseboat, even a large and luxurious one, or in any of the numerous *dak* bungalows along her various routes out of Srinagar; it is more likely she stayed in well-run hotels or as the guest of a local dignitary. Not that she was entirely averse to discomfort: the previous autumn, she had tried to reach Verinag Bagh by travelling along a direct but notoriously difficult route from Islamabad that ran for nineteen miles across rivers and rice fields, only to find her route blocked by flooding. On her second attempt, she and some friends accomplished the journey and, uncharacteristically, Constance camped out in the open air for several nights under the chenar trees.

Shalimar Bagh is a garden laid out in three separate sections, built in 1619 by the Mughal emperor Jahangir as a private enclosure for his wife Nur Jahan. This was where Constance engrossed herself in thorough research, taking copious notes and photographs, as well as sketching intensely. At the time of her visit, Shalimar was being maintained by HH the Maharaja of Jammu and Kashmir. Today, his example continues to be followed, although the garden is now a popular public park run by the local government. Constance expressed her fears for the survival of ancient Indian gardens and bemoaned their neglect, but most of them have survived and many have been, or are being, fully revived and restored, something for which she, as an early crusader for conserving the structures and the original planting, can be given some credit. At Shalimar, the outer garden lies closest to the lake, connected to it by a channel; the emperor's private garden is in the middle and, above it, the largest and prettiest of all, is the ladies' garden. Constance filled her sketchbook with drawings and worked up three of them as finished paintings for publication: *The Queen's Pavilion, On the Way to the Shalimar* (Fig 59) and *The Diwan-i-'Am* (Fig 60).

In her painting of the Diwan-i-'Am, the public garden, Constance included a vignette of the emperor seated on a small black marble throne

59   Constance Villiers Stuart, **On the Way to Shalimar**, 1912, original
watercolour, private collection

60   Constance Villiers Stuart, **The Diwan-I-'Am, Shalimar Bagh**, Plate XXIII, reproduced in *Gardens of the Great Mughals*, 1913

overlooking a fabulous waterfall which, when in full flow, formed a single sheet of water. It cascaded into a vast tank below, around which visitors thronged to see their ruler and gaze at the neat lines of fountains spouting forth more water and adding a refreshing zest to the atmosphere. It was an enchanting place, one which captivated Constance, who described it as having 'a subtle air of leisure and repose, ... and a romantic indefinable spell'. Her painting was taken from a sketch she had made on site (Fig 61) but, as at the Taj the year before, she made use of photography, too (Fig 62), although this time she did not paint a direct copy.

It was at a grand luncheon held at the Shalimar Gardens later in the year that Constance came across Brigadier-General Sir Percy Molesworth Sykes,[15] who was a keen amateur historian and author of several books as well as a soldier and diplomat. He had immersed himself in the study of Persian history and culture while serving as Consul in Kerman and, consequently, was of great interest to Constance, who naturally wanted to glean from him as much information as possible about Persian paradise gardens. Over consommé, canard sauvage, fruit au maraschino and fromage, their conversation turned from Isfahan to Delhi. In particular, the main topics of speculation were the Viceroy's future house and garden, and the question of where exactly they would be located. On the back of her menu, Constance scribbled down 'Various Sites: Raisina Hill and Talkatora'; she then wrote to Lord Hardinge in November, giving him her opinion on those locations. Lord Hardinge himself was actually in Kashmir at the same time as Constance, and possibly at the same luncheon as the guest of the Maharaja of Jammu and Kashmir who, despite being 'incoherent at certain times of the day until he had taken his opium pill', was an extremely generous host who lavished hospitality upon his British guests. Whether or not a conversation between Constance and Lord Hardinge had taken place in Srinagar, he replied to her letter thanking her for her suggestions for utilising Talkatora Bagh,

61   Constance Villiers Stuart, sketch for **The Diwan-I-'Am**, 1912, pencil

62   Unknown maker, **_Lower Pavilion at Nishat Bagh_**, 1912, hand-coloured
lantern slide, Kashmir

which was a run-down Mughal garden surrounded by the wooded hills of the Delhi Ridge, and saying that if the decision were made to build the viceregal residence above the garden, he would make use of her plan.

Constance continued her work, moving on to Nishat Bagh, on the eastern side of Lake Dal. This garden has twelve impressive terraces, one for each sign of the zodiac, reflecting an ancient belief in astrology, which she thought made it a more joyful and dramatic place than Shalimar Bagh. Within the colourful flowerbeds she identified a wide variety of plants – lilies, pelargoniums, roses, asters and cosmos – that formed a polychromatic backdrop to the foaming fountains and water chutes. The sound and movement of the water, together with the blaze of colour that greeted the visitor, was exceptionally arresting. Constance's first visit to the garden may have been in a *shikara*,[16] which was, aesthetically, the best way to enter it. Seen from a boat, the architecture and grounds silhouetted against the mountainous background would have given sightseers a full appreciation of Nishat Bagh's beauty. However, Constance is more likely to have arrived by car, the usual way most visitors in 1912 would have entered. She complained that approaching the garden from Lake Dal had been spoiled by the 'intrusion of the modern road'. Whichever way one chose to come into the garden, the spectacular sight on first encounter generally elicited a gasp of pleasure and surprise.

The Lower Pavilion at Nishat Bagh, where Constance set up her easel, was open at the back and front, allowing gentle breezes to carry the scent of flowers and enhance the cooling effect of the water. As she worked on her sketches, perfectly shaded in such amazing and fragrant surroundings, she must have thought she had stumbled upon a unique studio in an earthly paradise. (In recent years the rear and front openings have been enclosed, thus ruining the view, which now is best seen from the *zenana* terrace at the top level.) Constance came to Nishat Bagh at the right time to see the canals flowing and festooned with fountains, descending step by step to the lake below and edged by magnificently tall chenar trees. She made two detailed watercolour sketches of the Lower Pavilion (Hall of Fountains), showing the mountains in the background and coloured with soft blue, pink and grey tones, contrasting shadows with bright reflections of sunlight (Fig 63). One of these formed the basis of Plate XXV in *Gardens of the Great Mughals*. Interestingly, Constance hand-coloured a glass-plate slide to ensure she had an accurate record of the exactly the right tones (Fig 64).

Of special interest to Constance were the Kashmiri flower festivals around Lake Dal. These events were not only spectacles in themselves, but also places where so much could be learnt about different varieties of native plants. Lilacs, both Persian and European, every colour of narcissus, tulips, irises and lupins abound in spring, followed in the summer by another kaleidoscope, this time of roses, carnations, jasmine, hollyhocks, delphiniums, peonies and pinks. Iris motifs were particularly popular in decorative schemes for fabrics, tiles, stone and wood carvings, and Constance herself later included the species in the design on the cover of *Gardens of the Great Mughals*. She referred to the iris by its Kashmiri name, Gul-i-mazár ('flower of the graves'), because it was associated with the afterlife and planted around unmarked graves (Fig 65). Besides the knowledge she was acquiring, Constance enjoyed observing the daily life of Kashmiri people and singled out the Festival of the Roses as the place to catch a glimpse of family groups gossiping, smoking hookahs and picnicking on *nader-monja* (lotus stem fritters) accompanied by hot *kahwa* (Kashmiri tea) poured from traditional samovars. She was attracted to the sight of women and children draped in bright, diaphanous clothing sitting amid a colourful array of different roses, the best of which, Constance claimed, was the yellow Maréchal Niels.

Another impressive Kashmiri flower at its peak in July is the wild rose lotus, which floats on the surface of a lake and creates a great swaying haze of pink. So stunning was its appearance in the summer of 1912 that

63   Constance Villiers Stuart, *The Hall of Fountains*, 1912,
watercolour. Reproduced as Plate XXV in *Gardens of the Great
Mughals*, under the title *The Lower Pavilion, Nishat Bagh*

64   Constance Villiers Stuart, *The Hall of Fountains*, 1912, hand-coloured
lantern slide

65   Constance Villiers Stuart, **Sketch of Irises on Unmarked Kashmiri Graves**, 1912, pencil

on one occasion Constance rowed out into the middle of Lake Dal at dawn for an inimitable and unforgettable, almost spiritual, experience – to witness the tightly closed pink buds opening en masse in response to the light. As they are sacred symbols, enormous amounts of lotus flowers were harvested daily to be offered in the temples on holy days, or to decorate, in fabulous quantities, a maharaja's palace. There were practical uses, too; the stems and seed pods of the lotus are edible. They are still being sold in the bazaars and by itinerant fruit and vegetable sellers around the lake, exactly as they were when Constance was there.

Lotuses flowered equally abundantly at two other lakes, Manasbal Lake in the Jhelum Valley, and the huge Wular Lake[17] that lies about forty miles north of Srinagar on the Gulmarg Road, close to the little town of Sopore, then famed as the starting point of the beautiful Lolab Valley and celebrated for its fishing. Constance and Patrick visited the area together on one of their excursions around Kashmir. Darogha Bagh is a small Mughal garden at Manasbal, sometimes called Lalla Rookh's Garden, a place which might have been the motivation for the visit, but it appears that on this occasion research was not the main purpose of the Villiers Stuarts' trip. Instead, their time was allocated to recreation, sketching the lakes and surrounding water bean villages, boating, bird-watching and swimming in the clear, ice-cold water. They returned to Srinagar and Lake Dal to see one more small-scale garden, the delightful Chasma Shah (Chashme Shahi) built around a spring with reputed medicinal properties and lying adjacent to the Governor's House (Raj Bhavan). Their visit was recorded in a page from Constance's sketchbook which shows how she conducted her research (Fig 66). Notes are hurriedly scribbled across the paper, outlining the principal features of the garden, together with small pencil-drawn details and, on the facing page, a more fully delineated drawing.

Verinag Bagh, a favourite resort of Emperor Jahangir and Empress Nur Jahan, situated at the base of the Banihal Pass, was an important

66   Constance Villiers Stuart, a page from her sketchbook, showing the
garden at Chasma Shah, Kashmir, 1912, pencil

garden on the itinerary. It was known for, amongst other things, its forty-foot-deep octagonal tank crammed with sacred fish. Constance spent time there and painted a version of the tank showing the fish rushing to greet a sari-clad women who appears to be feeding them (Fig 67). This sketch was a contender for inclusion in *Gardens of the Great Mughals* but, in the final selection, another image was chosen (Fig 68), showing a fish leaping from the water as a kneeling woman feeds it. The viewpoint of the sketch allows the whole scene to be viewed from a distance and in a setting which reveals more of Verinag's architecture. Constance and Patrick stayed for a few quiet days of 'reading, writing and painting under the fruit trees' and experiencing 'the charm of solitude' at their temporary home, a wooden-latticed summer house. It is unusual for Constance to describe a personal recollection of place – she wanted to offer an objective account of Mughal gardens, not a memoir – but evidently Verinag made a deep impression on her, enough to recount picturesque details of what she saw: Brahmins gathering Persian roses for their shrine, pilgrims performing *pradakshina*,[18] and schoolboys studying their lessons in the shade and learning to swim in the stream.

When writing about Kashmir, Constance revealed her love of the region and its people, and how full of admiration she was for the physical beauty of the men and women she met or saw in passing. Good looks and beautiful garments were important to her wherever she went and could, in an instant, tilt her judgement in a person's favour. She appears not to have shared the almost universal British attitude of that era towards the inhabitants of Kashmir, which was one of extreme wariness and negativity. Early twentieth-century guidebooks gave harsh warnings to tourists, comparing Kashmiris unfavourably with Indians from other parts of the country. In contrast to Bengalis, Kashmiris were thought 'more robust and manly' because they had beards, took snuff and did not smoke, but these perceived qualities were overshadowed by their flaws: dirtiness, immoral habits and cunning, cheating ways. More bluntly, one author

67   Constance Villiers Stuart, **Woman feeding Fish at Verinag Bagh**,
1912, watercolour, Kashmir. This image was rejected in favour of **The
Octagonal Tank**, Plate XXVII, *Gardens of the Great Mughals*

68   Constance Villiers Stuart, **The Octagonal Tank**,
Plate XXVII, *Gardens of the Great Mughals*, 1913, from an
original watercolour

stated that a Kashmiri man 'is an accomplished liar and bigot; he is ... ignorant, dishonest, and intriguing. The long rule of the Afghan has left its mark and, from Gilgit to Jammu, unnatural vices help to make the Kashmiri a poor creature.'

Constance never visited Kashmir again but retained vivid nostalgic memories of it for the rest of her life. She and Patrick had been tremendously happy whenever they had been together there, sharing their sporting and artistic interests in a climate that suited them; they had not experienced the severity of winter, nor the challenges of summer heat, but had been accorded every luxury of accommodation and transport. With hindsight masking the grind of daily life for most Kashmiris, Constance's perception was forever rose-tinted and biased. Nevertheless, she had gained a great deal of knowledge and, in later years, when she was in her seventies and teaching flower arranging and floral art, she wistfully imparted what she knew of the region to her students, interjecting her instructions with personal reminiscences, such as the first time she had seen Crown Imperials growing wild near Baramulla. She remembered encountering blooms so large and numerous that the sight stopped her in her tracks and stuck in her mind forever. Unable to resist temptation, she brought some of these red and yellow lilies back to Norfolk, where they grew well in the woodlands and could be used as bold statement pieces in her demonstrations. She never failed to mention that the Crown Imperial was the favourite flower of the Mughal emperors, which is how it got its name.

Towards the end of October 1912, Constance drove to Simla (Shimla), partly to visit Pinjor Garden (Pinjore Garden or Yadavindra Garden) on the way. It nestled beside a stream in the foothills of the Himalayas, and she described it as the Mughal garden which was, compared with the others she had seen, the least changed of all. Before visiting Pinjor, her expectations of the garden had been low, a feeling reinforced by her first impressions as she drove through distinctly uninviting gates. However, she was pleasantly surprised to see what lay within the exterior walls at the very heart of the garden; she recorded seeing purple bougainvillaea tumbling from the parapets of old towers, quantities of unruly jasmine and untended roses mingling with palms lining the water's edge, and many varieties of unusual butterflies enhancing the scene. Colour and a romantic historical atmosphere made this semi-deserted, paradisiacal wilderness so seductive to a painter's eye. By climbing up and standing on top of one of the summer houses, Constance saw a stunning view across the countryside to Umballa (Ambala) and understood immediately why this site had been chosen. She had the good fortune to stay in a suite of rooms above the garden as the guest of the fabulously rich Maharaja of Patiala, Bhupinder Singh, who had recently married a new wife[19] amid much celebration and commotion. As the noisy and prolonged festivities began to wane, Constance could see the Maharaja's brightly uniformed staff through the heat-haze, smoking hookahs, relaxing and dozing beside the flowerbeds in a silence broken only by the call of peacocks and songbirds. With her penchant for frothy prose, she mentioned that, at that moment, she herself was artistically dressed in her painting outfit, a simple white muslin dress set off by a fashionable parasol held high above her head; she pictured herself starring in a scene in which she walked through an enchanted door to become part of an ancient Mughal miniature. It was just a figment of her lyrical imagination, not matched by the purely representational painting of Pinjor's splendid garden which she went on to produce, and even this record of a vivid memory is now sadly lost (Fig 69).

After such a productive time touring, studying and painting in India, Constance had finished all she could achieve within the period of Patrick's posting and, in the spring of 1913, the Villiers Stuarts returned to England. A & C Black agreed to publish Constance's proposed book, which she started to write as soon as she got back to Beachamwell Hall. Simultaneously, she began to solicit help from people of influence and

69   Constance Villiers Stuart, **Pinjor**, Plate XXXII, *Gardens of the Great Mughals*

audaciously wrote to Queen Mary, whom she revered, asking for permission to dedicate *Gardens of the Great Mughals* to her. Her request was politely declined by the Queen's lady-in-waiting, Lady Mary Trefusis, who softened the blow by saying that 'Her Majesty [would] be glad to accept a copy when it is published'. Perhaps aware of her overreach, when the time came Constance conferred the dedication upon her own mother. Surprisingly, after the book's publication, a magazine called *The Queen* printed a review which gave an enhanced impression of the contents of Lady Mary's rather curt letter:

> [Queen Mary], who is so well informed on all matters
> connected with India, its history and traditions, is much
> interested in the book that has just been brought out by
> Mrs Villiers Stuart, on the subject of the Imperial Gardens
> of India and … . Her Majesty has written to Mrs Villiers
> Stuart, through Lady Mary Trefusis, expressing her pleasure
> in the prospect of personally studying the book which is
> charmingly illustrated by sketches from the brush of the
> talented authoress.

Constance also approached Lord Hardinge. He seemed unaware of the impending publication when he wrote to her in the summer of 1913 in response to a renewed enquiry about his plans for the garden at Viceroy's House at New Delhi. He said he was delighted to hear that she 'was bringing out an illustrated book on modern Indian formal gardening' but that, at present, he had no ideas for his garden at New Delhi, which had not even been marked out at that point. He added: '… any ideas that your book will be able to convey to me and to those who will carry them out will indeed be very welcome'. He went on to say, 'I am hoping that we shall have a very copious water supply upon which, in Delhi, the future of gardens absolutely depends. The beautiful gardens we saw in Kashmir with their water and fountains greatly impressed me.' This refutes Constance's claim made in correspondence with the Institute of Landscape Architects (ILA) in the 1940s, and in a magazine interview in 1956, that Lord Hardinge had formally requested her to write a book about Mughal gardens.

The process of writing was not an easy one, and Constance admitted that the venture 'presented great difficulties' owing to her inexperience and having just six months in which to complete the manuscript. Her publishers, A & C Black, were exasperated with her and frequently reprimanded her for making extensive and expensive alterations to the text and for the tardiness of her responses to their questions and to meet their deadlines. She had offered to provide the index and a glossary, which she still had not done by the end of September, so the original publication date of October was then shifted to November.

These delays were compounded by her decision to expand the original brief to include information about Indian handicrafts and, in an attempt to bring contemporary relevance to her subject, by lobbying her readers to consider the 'bearing of Indian garden-craft on the pressing problem of New Delhi.' Having made her case for sympathy in the introduction, she then pleaded for the reader's understanding and leniency. The publishers no doubt added to her fears about the reception of *Gardens of the Great Mughals* by writing to her the week after the press copies were sent out, saying 'very little interest has been shown in your book so far but a few good reviews may help this'. In the event, anxiety was unnecessary because when the book came out, priced at 12s 6d,[20] it was favourably reviewed and, although some critics were condescending, the majority overflowed with praise not just for the text but also for the illustrations.

Constance published under the name C. M. Villiers Stuart. One of the first mistakes made by several reviewers was to assume that she was a man, which was possibly her intention. Perhaps she thought that a book about a serious subject written by a woman was less likely to sell well than one by a man. Some reviewers knew her gender and were complimentary but, simultaneously, they patronised her efforts, as in the *Royal Fusiliers Chronicle*, the magazine published by her husband's regiment, which stated: 'The author had the originality to escape from the groove in which many of her sex exist in our Great Eastern Dependency, where they take no interest in the country or the people, but spend their time in fruitless gossip at the Clubs, looking forward to supper … .' Another remarked that Constance had set an example to other expatriate women by showing them 'how to employ the compulsory inactivity of the life of an officer's wife'.

There was almost complete agreement on the quality of Constance's painting. Only two dissenters can be found among more than eighty reviews. The *Times Literary Supplement* observed that '[t]he colours in many of the drawings are deficient in tone, especially for a bright climate. She misses the range between the dark green foliage and the highlights on stone or marble'. *Gardeners' Chronicle* claimed that her watercolours, 'though pretty enough, [are] a trifle weak and perfunctory', but that, despite this, the book would still make 'an acceptable Christmas present'. The *Pioneer* was less flattering: after empathising with Constance's attraction to the beauty of India's old gardens, it criticised her flamboyant prose as 'dithyrambic' and claimed that:

> … the reader is apt to tire of pages in which the writer
> is everlastingly attitudinising for effect with shimmering
> streams of intoxicating phrases. And beyond all that too, in a
> mood which is called schwärmerisch (gushing), or something
> intensely sentimental, she dived into all sorts of underlying
> symbolism, against which, she confesses, she had been
> warned.

Most described the book in terms of femininity as 'exquisite', 'dainty', 'charming', 'delicate', 'enchanting' and 'delightful'. Some noted that the illustrations accorded well with the subject and others commended

Constance for her powers of observation and imagination. She had every reason to be satisfied with her achievement, especially when those among her mentors showed their appreciation. Sir George Birdwood, who was *the* establishment voice for India's art and culture in Britain at the time, having attained high rank at the India Museum (later incorporated into the Victoria and Albert Museum), wrote encouragingly in *Country Life*: '*The Gardens of the Great Mughals* was an inspiration of genius, and would always remain the definite, bright feather in her cap … . No one before Mrs Villiers Stuart, has ever written on the subject'. E. B. Havell, the influential arts administrator and author, was another firm supporter. He wrote to Constance privately, trying to allay some of her insecurities about the project: 'I don't think you have the least reason to fear that critics will either despise it or rend it to pieces. It comes at a most opportune moment and throws much light on a subject which has been totally neglected.' From November 1913 to April the following year, reviews appeared regularly in national and regional newspapers and journals across Great Britain, India and Ireland, including *The Times*, *Illustrated London News*, *Pioneer*, *Westminster Gazette*, *Studio*, *Spectator*, the *Yorkshire Post*, the *Liverpool Courier*, *Empire* magazine, *Tatler*, the *Times of India* and the *Irish Times*.

As the accolades poured in, invitations to lecture at prestigious venues followed, including from the Royal Society of Arts (RSA) and the Horticultural Club. On 19 March, at Number 8 John Adam Street, Covent Garden, Constance delivered a lecture titled 'Indian Water Gardens' to a crowded meeting of the RSA; it was one of her first public speaking engagements and she was in her element, lecturing about a subject on which few were as informed as she was, let alone had had any firsthand experience. The chairman, Sir Steuart Bayley, a former Lieutenant Governor of Bengal, introduced her talk, mentioning that it would be accompanied by 'lantern views'. Constance spoke eloquently on her practiced themes: the architectonic genius of the Mughals, the brilliance of their horticulture, the ruination of Indian gardencraft by English influences and the possibilities presented by the construction of New Delhi, all of which she handled with 'great charm and clearness'. Her comments were well received, but Sir Steuart felt she had been overly harsh on the British and suggested that the decay of Mughal gardening had been caused by political upheavals preceding British rule. Mr Abbas Ali Baig of the India Council agreed with Constance, saying that beautifying the new capital in conformity with the tradition and sentiments of Indian people was not only realisable, it was also very desirable.

The guest list was extensive and included the eminent garden historian, Constance's friend and Norfolk neighbour, Alicia Amherst (by then styled Mrs Evelyn Cecil); another neighbour, Prince Frederick Duleep Singh, and his sister Sophie Duleep Singh; Sir Krishna Gupta, an Indian barrister and civil servant; the poet Mrs Sarojini Naidu; Constance's mentor E. B. Havell; the Indian-born writer and British administrator, Sir Richard Temple; and numerous others. The press enjoyed the occasion and were quite smitten with Constance, who was described by the *Lady* as 'a young and attractive woman, [who] looked well in her black dress with white frilled vest … . Her Indian friends were delighted to recognise nestling in her black lace hat the White Lotus of Evening, the symbolic touch being much appreciated.' However, more soberingly, in response to Constance's plea for the gardens of New Delhi to reflect and preserve Mughal gardencraft, the *Pioneer* ended its review of 18 April 1914 with the withering comment: 'whatever style the Government may build at Delhi, the gardens are not likely to be a disgrace. One of the architects is Mr. Lutyens, who is an architectural gardener of such reputation that it is unlikely he has anything to learn from the gifted authoress of *Gardens of the Great Mughals*.'

A month later Constance repeated her lecture, with variations, at the Horticultural Club in London. It is significant that Lady Hardinge attended, just two months before her untimely death. She was in total agreement with Constance regarding the need for Mughal gardens to be at the heart of the design for the Viceroy's House and it has been suggested that the two of them, together with Gertrude Jekyll,[21] had first embedded this seed of an idea in Lutyens's mind.[22] Coincidentally, the Horticultural Club lecture took place during the opening week of an exhibition at the Royal Academy of Arts showing the architectural watercolour drawings of the government centre of the new capital city of New Delhi. The designs for New Delhi were of mainstream, topical interest and much discussed over the ensuing two decades. What was supposed to have taken four years to finish took over seventeen, with the house and garden being completed in 1929 and inaugurated with New Delhi as a whole in 1931, sixteen years before Indian Independence and the Act of Partition in 1947.

By offering suggestions as to how the traditional concept might be applied in a contemporary way to the Viceroy's new garden, Constance had certainly played her part in raising the profile of Mughal gardens at an apposite moment. Her contribution was recognised when she was awarded the RSA's silver medal in 1914, but she had not achieved what she had really wanted, which was to be recognised in some capacity as an official advisor on the design and implementation of the New Delhi gardens. What she lost in international prestige, she gained closer to home. Constance's lectures and the reviews of *Gardens of the Great Mughals*, in particular the one by Sir George Birdwood, seem to have served as the foundation for a very successful relationship with *Country Life* (the magazine in which the Birdwood review appeared) that would span more than forty years. She had also produced a book of lasting value and appeal, which is still consulted and regularly cited today, over one hundred years after it was published.

CHAPTER SIX

1914–1918: World War I

Buoyed by the critical success of *Gardens of the Great Mughals*, Constance wanted to capitalise on her newfound celebrity, but timing was not on her side. During the first half of 1914, Britain was on the brink of war with Germany and opportunities of the type she was interested in – art, history and gardens – were few. Once war was declared later that year, Constance, notoriously ambitious and not easily thwarted, managed to turn the situation to her advantage by continuing to write; she focused her attention on journalism, where she found a market principally, but not exclusively, at *Country Life* for articles about India and gardens as well as the occasional book review. But it was in April 1915, when the 2nd Battalion Royal Fusiliers landed at Gallipoli, that she devised a way to do what she really liked best: to combine her love of travel with an element of risk and write about it. Patrick arrived in Gallipoli to join his battalion in August 1915 as part of the Allied powers' attempt to aid Serbia against an attack from Germany, Bulgaria and Austria-Hungary. Just as Constance had optimised her experience of being 'a trailing spouse' in India, she saw that her husband's military career could once again provide her with a chance for personal growth and advancement. Against all advice to the contrary, she would embark on a dangerous journey to join Patrick at Salonica (Thessalonica) the following year, not just to be with reunited with him, but to be part of the action. Over the course of her journey, she would succeed in reinventing herself as an anonymous 'woman correspondent' reporting on conditions in the region, while also writing under her own name about the flowers and gardens of Macedonia. For Constance, a life of adventure trumped one of domesticity and motherhood every time. Her letters from Salonica to Beachamwell Hall would show that although she loved her mother and daughter deeply, she did not have any qualms about leaving them behind in the middle of a war to pursue her own interests.

Before she left England, Constance applied herself diligently to becoming a recognised journalist, homing in on *Country Life* with the help of her brother-in-law Gerald Villiers Stuart, who had in the past occasionally written for the magazine about rural life in Ireland. Her first assignment, 'Indian Garden Palaces', published on 12 June 1915, was a five-page overview of Nishat Bagh, Shalimar Bagh and Deeg Palace illustrated with black and white photographs. Her paean to India's historic architecture and horticulture included an introduction which, even for the time, seems naive. In it, she praises the country's nobility for offering their troops to assist the British in the First World War:

> The response of India to her Emperor in his hour of need
> will always remain one of the most splendid pages in the
> history of the European War. The names of the Maharajas
> and Nawabs lending aid read like some great Homeric list.
> The active devotion of all classes to the King-Emperor –
> the embodiment of their country's unity – has proved as
> inspiring to the whole Empire as it has been disconcerting to
> its enemies.

It was the first of over thirty articles that Constance would write for *Country Life*, albeit with occasional long gaps between them. The next one, a review of a book called *Rajput Painting*, by Ananda Coomaraswamy, did not appear until April 1916, by which time she was already in Greece.

In a series of moving letters to his mother-in-law from the Macedonian front, Patrick shows himself to be an extremely devoted husband, doting father and a conscientious custodian of the Beachamwell estate, upon whom Frances, in particular, leant heavily for guidance and advice. In one of his first letters, written on 9 September 1915, perhaps fearing for his life in the early days of the campaign, he thanks Frances for all her goodness to him over the past decade and reassures her that his life is much less mentally and physically exhausting and hazardous than when he first landed on 'that never to be forgotten morning of 7th August'. He describes the shelling and the trenches as having become monotonous but expresses gratitude for not being overworked or underfed. He enquires about the tenants on the estate and whether there is any loss of income needing to be addressed; he enlivens his correspondence with snippets of information for Constance's benefit about the beauty of the countryside, trees and wildflowers, mosque architecture and the way in which each house in every village was decorated with colourful plants in terracotta pots. In conclusion, he begs Frances and Constance not to worry about his safety, but then swiftly retracts the remark by saying that 'it does not pay to say one is safe because often death follows as the words are written'.

Patrick was fortunate in having his own servant,[23] Private Playford, also from Norfolk, with whom he got on well. In addition to having someone to take care of his uniform, clean his boots and prepare his meals, Patrick had the privilege of receiving regular deliveries from Beachamwell of assorted 'necessities': new gumboots, two smoke helmets, cake, chocolate, tinned fruit, cigarettes and cigars. Much as he liked these surprise hampers and useful presents they were, under the circumstances, embarrassing. He admonished Constance for her extravagance and asked her to cancel a standing order of luxury food from Fortnum and Mason, with the assurance that the Royal Fusiliers were well provided for by the Army and Navy Stores. He added a cautionary note, recommending that Frances and Constance exercise the greatest economy in the light of enormously increased taxation in Britain.

No amount of material advantage or social status could prevent feelings of homesickness and longing for family and friends that afflicted all those at war, and Patrick, who was unashamedly emotional, was no exception. Like many others, he complained about the behaviour and incompetence of some of his superiors and grieved for the loss of men he knew, but he balanced his sad or angry words with recognition of his blessings, knowing he could have been sent to an even more dangerous theatre of war elsewhere in Europe. With touching simplicity he always included little notes for Patricia, telling her, for instance, that he was collecting rare Turkish stamps for her, or that he was sleeping in a cosy tent which even she, at five years old, would not be able to stand up in.

Patrick saw plenty of action and always wrote home quickly to quell his wife's fears after any event that might be misreported in the British press, as happened in December 1915 when the Fusiliers came under heavy attack. He wrote, in what he called a self-censored mail, to correct errors in newspaper coverage and to say that the Bulgars, despite having uniforms similar to those of the Royal Fusiliers, were 'formidable looking ruffians' whose astonishing size and physique impressed the British, as did their artillery and the accuracy of their shelling. The Fusiliers' Brigade HQ had to depart hurriedly from their position on the Kosturino Ridge,[24] move silently down a ravine, and leave most of their belongings behind.[25] Other brigades also started to retire as the Bulgars 'swarmed up over the top [of the Doiran Ridge] … with their peculiar piercing cheer ringing through the night as our last Companies got away'. Patrick called the retreat, after having been 'greatly outnumbered and lucky to escape', an 'exciting and interesting experience'. At the time, he believed the enemy was following the retreating soldiers and he feared that the Siege of Salonica might be imminent. Nervous also of reprisals for his vivid description of the battle, he ended by saying, 'I expect that I have told you more than I ought to have.' A few days later he wrote from a peaceful and beautiful part of Macedonia to say: 'One almost looks back with regret at the exciting last day in Serbia. We shall no more exchange shots with the Bulgar patrols in Kosturino or warm ourselves in adjacent houses in the Ormanli by mutual agreement.' For his part in the retreat, in which the Brigade did well and bore the brunt of the fighting, Patrick was mentioned in dispatches by his superior officer, Brigadier Nicol.

In early February 1916, Patrick was becoming increasingly anxious because Constance had told him that she intended to travel to Greece to see him and was on the point of leaving. He was afraid that if there was a bombardment, Salonica would be set ablaze because most of the houses were constructed of timber[26] (Fig 70). He wrote to Frances stressing that he was against Constance coming to stay at the front line, but if she refused to be dissuaded and if he could get away from camp for a week, then perhaps she would agree to a compromise – to meet in Athens, which was officially neutral territory. Unfortunately, Constance had left England before Patrick received an answer to his request for leave, which, in the event, was turned down. He wrote forlornly to Frances, saying, 'She is nearly sure to come here and I don't suppose anything I could have said would have stopped her.' Yet he was conflicted, adding: 'I frankly do not like the idea of her travelling in these uncertain times, although my own desire to see her again makes it difficult for me to urge her very strongly not to come.'

Constance had obtained special permission to travel abroad and took a route from Calais, via Paris, Marseilles, Messina – which she loathed because of its 'malign sort of air' – and Naples to Athens. The small boat in which she had sailed the final leg had given its passengers 'a frightful bucketing about [and] pitched and tossed for all it was worth. ... It was too rough to dress or to eat anything for two nights and a day', conditions Constance appears to have taken in her stride. Having sent

70   Constance Villiers Stuart, **Wooden Eaves**, Salonica,
1916, pencil and coloured crayon

telegrams to her worried mother from every city and port, she finally reached her destination in early March and stayed for a few days at the Palace Hotel in Athens, from where she wrote to Frances recalling the arrival at the port of Piraeus, which reminded her of India:

> We got in … just at sunset and the temples showed gold against the purple shadows creeping up the mountain. Like the Taj, they do not belie their reputation and the cypress trees everywhere – planted by the Turks I expect – make a wonderful contrast of colour and tone. The square in front of the Kings Place has a little grove of orange trees and lines of very old cypresses. It looks rich and beautiful, just what our stupid people ought to carry out in India – only they don't.

Wherever she went, Constance was bolstered by a network of useful, influential contacts. In Athens she had the support of Rear Admiral Hubert Cardale,[27] who managed her onward journey to Salonica, and of his wife, who provided her with introductions to various French and British women living there either as privileged military wives or working for the Red Cross. She took the slow boat from Athens and stopped en route for fifteen hours at Volo (Volos), which she described as 'a little town', although it is now a bustling port and industrial centre. There she took her 'first beautiful walk up the mountainside' with an American journalist and picked scarlet anemones and grape hyacinth, before creeping into Salonica 'through the mine fields led by a torpedo boat', only to find that her papers were not in order 'on account of some blunder of the Captain's'. She was rescued by the aide-de-camp of another British contact, Major Villiers, the Provost Marshal,[28] who turned up in a boat and took her away 'in triumph'.

Constance was made to feel welcome when, with a certain amount of fanfare, she eventually arrived at the port of Salonica, where 'even the General who feels he ought to disapprove of such an adventure' offered to show her the sights of the town. After their separation of almost eight months, Patrick and Constance were thrilled to be together again, to the point where they were both so excited that they could hardly talk to each other collectedly. Inevitably, their reunion caused resentment within the ranks and led to more requests for other wives to be allowed to visit, citing Mrs Villiers Stuart's example. Constance also discovered that Patrick's leave had been denied because the senior staff had feared accusations of favouritism. Some of the criticism was justified, because there had been preferential treatment: Constance had been entrusted with carrying government dispatches from Athens for delivery to the British Consul in Salonica, which helped expedite her journey. Besides that, her many boxes of luggage were not searched at all after she left England, which was unusual during wartime.

Once settled in the Hotel Splendide, her home for the duration of her stay, Constance remarked that the difficulties of the journey faded into insignificance as she began to explore the area and meet people. While Patrick was working hard supervising brigade training, inspecting the English trenches and dealing with administrative work, she gravitated towards the French expatriate community, among whom were 'a number de bonne famille doing various odd jobs', including the Comtesse Marie de Chabannes la Palice with whom she frequently walked in the mountains. Together they discovered the ruins of Turkish gardens, looked for wildflowers and explored many of the 350 little ancient churches in the town, most of which were crowded with refugees. Constance thought that Macedonia was desolate and considered its faith, the dust, abandoned buildings and personal insecurity of its inhabitants redolent of the Middle Ages. Yet it was interesting, too, with much to discover; she enjoyed wandering through the maze of narrow streets and lanes, chancing upon domed Byzantine churches and being surprised by glittering mosaics within. There was a frisson of excitement about the city, heightened by the war. With its crowded cafés and bazaars, scattered fragments of classical pillars, capitals and eerily deserted ruins sitting incongruously alongside the bustle of disembarking troops at the harbour and the commotion of cargo being unloaded along the quays, Salonica was never dull.

There were moments when the war impinged on Constance's safety. Writing to her mother on 29 March 1916, she revealed: '… we have had a real bombardment here. Bombs fell all round us, but curiously one feels more cross than actually afraid.' Seemingly of more concern to her was being woken up and having to get dressed in order to evacuate the hotel. This perceived inconvenience was compounded by the loss of a pair of expensive buckled shoes which she subsequently 'missed dreadfully'. Quite impervious to danger, Constance shrugged off the aerial bombardment but admitted that she was 'glad to be able to say [she] had come under fire'. Soon after the emergency was over, she resumed regular activities – socialising, horse riding, sightseeing, looking for mosaics, writing, drawing and painting – with her usual single-mindedness and independence.

Over a period of a month, she created a charming set of little coloured drawings sketched for pleasure during exploratory walks which give little hint of her proximity to action. Her chief subject was architecture, and it appears that she was just as interested in portraying the backstreets of Salonica, which reminded her of Srinagar, as she was in the more well-known ecclesiastical and civic buildings. The Old Town – Constance called it 'the Jewish Town' – with its atmosphere of antiquity and cosmopolitan blend of religions and languages, appealed to her greatly.[29] This is evident in *Side Street in Salonique* (Fig 71), which depicts a crumbling old building beside a rough, unmade road, a Turkish carpet airing from one of its windowsills, wisteria tumbling wildly over a wall and a darkly clad figure walking into the distance, together creating the illusion of a mediaeval scene. She made two versions of this view. The other, very similar, is entitled *In the Turkish Town* and, verso, inscribed *The Hepta-pyrgion*. As well as architecture, Constance was attracted by traditional

71   Constance Villiers Stuart, **Salonique** or (verso) ***A Side
Street, Salonique In the Jewish Town***, 1916, pencil and
coloured crayon

national dress, which had been a fascination since childhood. She noted: 'The costumes of the Spanish Jewesses make them look like … portraits by Rembrandt. I suppose it must be the only case in Europe where the costume of the merchant classes has survived from those days. But this isn't really Europe.'

One of Constance's sketches, made on the spot using pencil and coloured crayon, was of the White Tower, once a Byzantine fortress, rebuilt by the Ottomans in the fifteenth century as a prison, then remodelled and whitewashed in 1912, since when it has stood as a symbol of the city. Before sitting down to sketch, Constance climbed the 'interminable stone stairs' to see a garden being built by British sailors on the battlements. Some naval signallers had brought earth and stones from some distance away and hoisted them into place. 'And there', she noted, 'high above the curious cosmopolitan crowd which gathers round the tower on band days, they hope to grow some fine sweet peas.' Constance's drawing rendered the tower from a low viewpoint, obliterating the top turret from view; she also created an imaginary rural setting, emphasised by the inclusion of a mule carrying a heavy load up a grassy incline towards the tower (Fig 72). This is not how the tower was represented in most postcards of the era, which show it adjacent to the harbour, surrounded by a *chemise*, or apron wall,[30] along which people strolled wearing western clothes of the period. Other sketches in the same medium feature exteriors and interiors of churches and mosques. Constance's quickly executed drawings focused on these places of timeless sanctuary to create a mood of peace, perhaps intentionally as an antidote to war. Two interiors, *Holy Wisdom* (Fig 73) and *The Red Pillar* (Fig 74), draw attention to the richly decorated walls and ceilings by highlighting the architectural details. Her exterior views of buildings include *Church of the Holy Apostles* (Fig 75), a drawing of the fourteenth-century church which later became a mosque known for its impressive mosaics and frescos and which remains a major tourist attraction today.

72   Constance Villiers Stuart, untitled, Salonica, 1916,
pencil and coloured crayon

73 Constance Villiers Stuart, **Holy Wisdom**, 1916,
pencil and coloured crayon

74   Constance Villiers Stuart, **The Red Pillar**, 1916,
pencil and coloured crayon

75   Constance Villiers Stuart, **Church of the Holy
Apostles**, 1916, pencil and coloured crayon

Equally historically important is the Roman Arch of Galerius, which Constance drew in close-up detail, accentuating the sculptural qualities of the lower walls (Fig 76). The panels of the columns serve a narrative as well as a decorative function, depicting battle scenes and events from the life of Emperor Galerius. By giving her drawing the title *Coming in from the Country*, Constance humanises the grand scale of the monument and shows it not just as an iconic attraction and meeting place but also as a part of normal daily life. The humble mule, accompanied through the arch by three figures, perhaps heading for market, when set against the carved representations of Persian soldiers on rearing horses in the midst of a battle against Roman forces, makes a poignant contrast between the quotidian and the drama of combat. It is possible that Constance was making a connection between the fighting of Emperor Galerius in the fourth century and the war in and beyond Salonica in 1916.

The final work in the set of pencil and coloured crayon drawings was *The Clock-Tower Mosque* (Fig 77), an ambiguous sketch of a flight of steps leading into an unseen building in an unidentified location. On the left, a path leads to an archway where two figures – one seated, one standing – appear to be engaged in conversation. It raises the question of whether Constance was preparing this group of drawings, primarily of architectural details, for some sort of didactic display. She mounted them, which she rarely did with other sketches, and wrote titles prominently on the recto of most images, suggesting she may have been thinking of showing them in a gallery rather than publishing them in a magazine article.

As summer approached and her time in Salonica was coming to an end, Constance began planning how, once back in England, she could best use what she had seen and learned in Macedonia. She had received definite interest from newspapers and journals for reports about the war because she had made known her on-the-spot, firsthand experience. Her first commission came about quite by chance. Constance had made friends with several French and British women whom she had

76   Constance Villiers Stuart, *Coming in from the Country*, 1916, pencil and coloured crayon

THE CLOCK-TOWER MOSQUE.

77   Constance Villiers Stuart, **The Clock-Tower Mosque**, 1916, pencil and coloured crayon

seen regularly at local hospitals while they were volunteering with the Red Cross.[31] On one such visit, she noticed with admiration that the soldiers were creating gardens within the hospital precincts. After she had seen the 'timid flower borders emerge' around the Lembet Camp, which housed refugees, and witnessed the French *poilus*[32] planting salads, vegetables and herbs to alleviate food shortages among the Allied forces including the sick and wounded, Constance conceived of an idea for an interesting article, which she intended to write shortly after her return to Beachamwell Hall in July 1916.

The result was 'Photographed from an Aeroplane: Soldiers' Gardens round Salonica', published in the 5 August 1916 edition of *Country Life*. The article describes the efforts of the English, French and Greeks to plant neat potagers to produce food for hospital staff and soldiers, and to create flower beds to boost the morale of patients. Loyal as ever to India, Constance made special mention of Hospital Number Four, which was a field hospital for the troops of the various Indian Mule Corps. The native orderlies had devised and designed a large red cross out of poppies which they had dug up from the neighbouring meadows and planted at the hospital. A silver gelatin print (Fig 78) shows the gardeners at the same hospital, alongside nurses and the wounded, laying out more flower beds in front of makeshift wards. Constance praised the dedication of the French for creating such attractive and inspiring flowerbeds together with more practical, but still ornamental, vegetable patches, saying: 'If the British share the Turkish love of flowers, the French are especially skilful at laying out gardens. *Le prestige du dessin* as the saying goes, is the first concern of even camp gardeners. Our joy in the colour of flowers is balanced by the French feeling for form.' This sentiment is epitomised by the aerial shot showing hospital tents encircled by 'living pictures' of patriotic slogans and symbols made entirely of locally grown wisteria, roses, white lilies, violets, narcissi, carnations and jasmine (Figs 79 and 80).

78   Unknown, **Hospital Number Four, Salonica**, 1916,
selenium-toned silver gelatin print

79   Unknown, *Gloire À Notre France Eternelle*, 1916,
selenium-toned silver gelatin print

80   Unknown, *In the Aviation Camp*, 1916,
selenium-toned silver gelatin print

Constance's article also outlines the beautiful wildflowers on the hills surrounding Salonica which were 'constant sources of interest to our men'. It struck her as unusual that the 'most unexpected people start making collections and sending home bulbs and seeds'. She herself was very intrigued by the new and fascinating rock plants she found, as well as the 'home flowers' growing wild in Macedonia; she also admired the 'charming oriental custom of carrying a single flower for its perfume … .' noting '… the partly veiled women and the picturesque figures of the men as they walk along holding their rose or narcissus looking for all the world as if they had just stepped from the pages of a prized folio of Mughal portrait miniatures'.

Constance kept up her journalistic momentum. Two weeks later, *Country Life* published another of her commentaries, this time one that harked back to India. 'Three Kashmir Flowers' was an informative and charming essay about irises, wild roses and lotuses. Even in wartime, India was still at the forefront of British consciousness and readers could savour Constance's vivid descriptions of each flower and its uses and meaning in Indian decorative art, on tiles, curtains, lattices and beams. Then, in the penultimate year of the war, after Salonica had suffered a devastating fire, *The Times* commissioned Constance to share her experiences of living in the city before it was largely destroyed. This tragic event left 70,000 mostly Jewish people homeless and more than 9,500 homes, predominantly of wooden construction, razed to the ground. *The Times* wanted a nostalgic feature that captured the historic atmosphere of the city, something Constance was eminently well placed to deliver.

Published on 27 August 1917, and written in her customary elaborate style, Constance evokes the image of a city within a city, contrasting the busy modern waterfront with the old city on the hill above the Via Egnatia where, she says, 'the Moslem Salonica dreams apart'. Referencing veiled figures, Spanish Jewesses, beautiful clear-cut profiles, old slaves, chief dervishes, Anglo-Syrian merchants, descendants of the last Seljuk sultans and Muslim poets and scholars, Constance illuminated the city's cultural diversity and also her ability to befriend people of all faiths and backgrounds. She described going to the Turkish quarter with two companions, one a male translator, when it was considered dangerous for Westerners to do so. Her mission was to interrogate the Chief Dervish about the symbolism employed in the planting of Muslim tombs. After making salaams, being ushered onto a divan surrounded by animal skins strewn haphazardly across the floor and offered coffee and cigarettes, they embarked on a lengthy animated conversation that 'surged up and down in rich guttural tones' but which ultimately provided her with no new information at all.

The war had raised Constance's profile and benefited her reputation. She had branded herself as a daring woman willing to travel and take risks solely to further her specialist knowledge of architecture and horticulture, particularly that of the Muslim world. By expanding her scope from 'a journal for all interested in country life and country pursuits' to a national newspaper, she gained a significantly wider readership and became better known. Once Constance was re-established in England, she drew additional positive public attention by being headlined as one of the 'Society Ladies who are doing War Work'. She joined the Red Cross and began nursing at the Countess of Dundonald's Hospital in Belgravia, where she threw herself into the role with so much energy and devotion that Patrick and Frances feared she would injure her own health.

Although Constance was making a name for herself and advancing her career by dint of her own hard work, she could not have done so had she not been cushioned by a private income, which she took entirely for granted and considered her birthright. However, the war had changed everything and there were warning signs that all was not well behind the scenes. Sales of *Gardens of the Great Mughals* had been negatively affected by the war, something the publishers had not fully anticipated. At the outset, the book had done well from early to mid-1914 but, after August, when public priorities shifted to the war in Europe, interest slumped, and A & C Black were left with 1,500 copies on their hands. Adam Black appealed to Constance to do more to raise awareness and help sell more copies; the firm had already reduced the price to six shillings,[33] which was roughly half the original price and, in their opinion, 'dirt cheap'. Now they asked Constance to get in touch with Edwin Lutyens to offload the book because 'it would serve as most excellent propaganda'. Closer to home, Frances and Patrick were extremely worried about the maintenance of the Beachamwell estate, worries which, for whatever reason, never seemed to impact Constance. Patrick wrote to Frances with his usual pragmatism in 1917:

> I feel so much for your anxieties with regard to B'well – it
> is not easy to decide what is best to do; if however you get
> a reasonable offer for part of the estate you would be well
> advised to sell. I should be inclined to sell up to half of
> it, if the opportunity offers. Land, like coalmines will be
> nationalised in a few years and you will be bought out … ,
> that is one reason why I am not averse to selling part of the
> estate now, though I feel it to be the greatest pity to break
> up such an estate. … I am afraid the papers and politicians
> have been hoodwinking the people as to the possibility of a
> decisive victory against Germany; no such thing is possible
> under another two years of war. By that time a general
> sequestration of capital and property will be necessary to
> provide the necessary funds.

With society in a state of flux, the following decade promised to be a challenging one for Frances and the Villiers Stuarts.

CHAPTER SEVEN

Early Post-War and the Spanish Years

▲
▼

Constance experienced a long hiatus in productivity after the end of the war. Life became more domesticated, quieter and less adventurous. It is probable that Frances Fielden exerted some pressure on the couple. By then in her late sixties, and although happy with her role as a grandmother, she no longer wanted to be Patricia's surrogate parent and disciplinarian, nor the matriarch in sole charge of staff, tenants and large swathes of land. She fully expected Constance and Patrick to take responsibility for Patricia and to oversee the Beachamwell estate. This played out well for a while, but it was not to last. By the second half of the 1920s, Constance was restless and eager to follow her own interests again. Conflicted by wanting the best for her daughter and not wishing to take advantage of her mother, Constance nevertheless missed the intellectual stimulation and independence of travelling, researching, writing and painting. When the time came, she had a solution: Patrick could stay at home, run estate business and provide emotional support for Frances and Patricia, while she went abroad to work on another book. As a logical sequel to *Gardens of the Great Mughals*, she chose as her next subject the Moorish gardens of Spain. This would necessitate long periods travelling alone, accompanied only by her chauffeur, suitcases full of black clothes,[34] painting and photographic equipment and a new list of distinguished introductions.

Before resuming her travelling life, Constance stayed in England for several years but continued to be heavily involved in Indian causes. During the early Twenties, Britain's ties with India remained strong. The British were still required there for work, with eager new hopefuls regularly setting sail from Southampton and Tilbury for a future in South Asia. There were the 'old India hands' who had been resident for a long time, loved the lifestyle and wanted to stay on.[35] Those who returned to Britain were often nostalgic and tried to influence policy on the subcontinent from home by clinging on to relationships with family and friends they had left behind. Constance, along with other former expatriates, took on a new role by joining the Indian Women's Education Association based in London. The IWEA was set up to lobby for the franchise for Indian women and to promote girls' literacy at a time when only 1 per cent of female children in India could read and write. Constance was appointed the Honorary Organising Secretary to the Association and, as such, had to arrange lectures, petitions and fund-raising. She was part of a glamorous coterie of upper-class women with genuine philanthropic intentions and experience of living in India, for whom charitable work was a customary and socially acceptable occupation. One of the group was the determined and forceful Lady Willingdon,[36] a near contemporary of Constance's, whose husband was the Governor of Madras at the time and later would be Viceroy of India.[37] He described his wife as a constant source of support and encouragement, but other people called her domineering and egocentric. Another member was Lady Chelmsford, who had succeeded Lady Hardinge as Vicereine of India and shared her interests in the welfare of women and children, especially their health and education. Prominent feminist, writer and suffragist, Millicent Garrett Fawcett, was also connected with the Association through her presidency of the National Union of Women's Suffrage Societies.[38] These women and their numerous supporters campaigned diligently in Britain and India to change the law and create better opportunities for India's female population. Yet, in the *Times of India*, Lady Chelmsford revealed a surprisingly narrow range of aspirations for the women she wanted to help. She declared that, after five years in India and through her personal observations, 'The mass of Indian women, untouched as yet by our schools, [need to] be educated … to give them a sense of communal interest and responsibility, a desire for better homes, and enough elementary instruction to enable simple household affairs to be managed.' Constance had higher hopes, but was perhaps referring only to the elite when she wrote:

> Those who see below the surface in India know that the
> women have the power, for they hold the links with the past
> in their hands, and only with their help can their country
> be modernised without losing more than she gains in the
> process. Every artist in the East sees that very clearly. … It is
> just here, where practical statesmen so often fail, that women
> may prove the better guides; for like poets and artists, they
> rely on intuitive reasoning.

Constance had a knack for public relations, which she used energetically to benefit the IWEA; she was also well aware of the personal benefits of publicity, which brought her into the limelight again. For instance, when, in the early 1920s, she met Princess Mary at the Royal Free Hospital and presented three female Indian medical students to her, the occasion was widely reported in the national press, which added lustre to Constance's reputation as a doyenne of Anglo-Indian relations. Later, she held an At Home for Lord Lytton, Governor designate of Bengal,[39] and Lady Lytton. *The Times* devoted several columns to this, highlighting the impressive set of influential people who had been engaged to maximise the Association's reach. Among the guests was Sir Mancherjee Bhownaggree, a notable British politician of Indian Parsi heritage. As a member of the Conservative Party, he was already well known as a campaigner for change in India, especially for his consistent lobbying for improvements in vocational training and literacy instruction. In this capacity, he had agreed to chair the committee for Constance and to establish another one in Calcutta to raise more funds for the IWEA. The purpose of engaging Lord Lytton was to encourage him, on his return to India, to raise money and support for education within the country itself – a request to which he willingly acceded. Sir Mancherjee stated that 'The Indians were naturally a proud people, [and] the time was past when they could be regarded as not knowing what was good for them.' Constance herself occasionally failed to recognise this salient point. She had written to the Sultan Jahan Begum, head of the princely state of Bhopal (now part of Madhya Pradesh) who had befriended the Villiers Stuarts when they lived in India, and asked her for advice and financial assistance for the IWEA. Unfortunately, Constance had made some unintentionally offensive assertions in her letter to the Begum, who replied politely, yet firmly:

> I am afraid I do not agree with the view that Purdah is nothing more than a social custom. For the Mussulmans the custom is based on the explicit injunctions of our Holy Book – the Quran, which is the foundation of the Moslem faith. … Your Association will, I think be interested to know that, in my opinion, the Purdah system … is no hindrance, but a help to the discharge of all duties of social and political life, and to the attainment of high ideals of citizenship.

There were many other eminent men and women that attended the At Home for Lord and Lady Lytton – including Princess Sophia Duleep Singh, Sir Dhunjibhoy Bomanjee and Lady Bomanjee, Lady Mond and Dr Kate Platt (who, as the first Principal of Lady Hardinge Medical College, a training establishment in New Delhi specifically for Indian women to study medicine, showed just how much could be achieved through group efforts) – and Constance can take credit for raising the profile of the Association, bringing it to a wider audience, steering her coevals to a consensus of opinion and galvanising them into action. Her talent for persuasion might have led her into a more public and political role had her artistic bent not been so prominent. Her inclination lay elsewhere, as she admitted later in life: 'If I had been a man, I should have been an architect. But I am a woman, so I paint, write, take photographs and travel.'

Despite Frances's hopes to the contrary, the Villiers Stuarts returned to India in February 1924, but it was just for a short visit of no more than two months. Since Patrick is not listed as having been in India with the Royal Fusiliers during this period, they went for pleasure and an army reunion in Jullundur (now Jalandhar). The journey was largely undocumented, with Constance's sketchbook providing the only record of time spent in Karnal, East Punjab (later Haryana) and various cities in Rajasthan. Her first watercolour drawing (Fig 81) was quickly and roughly made at Chachrauli Palace, Karnal (now a ruin more commonly known as Chhachhrauli Fort), showing an unidentified woman seated beside an open window in the Hall of Private Audience, the receiving area for distinguished guests. At the time, the palace was occupied by the Maharaja Ravisher Singh and his wife, who could conceivably have been the sitter, although there is no evidence that Constance met the Maharani or her husband. Shortly afterwards, Constance travelled to Bharatpure (Bharatpur) and made a side-view sketch of the main entrance into the Ashtadhatu Gate at the massive, Jat-built,[40] seemingly indestructible and impenetrable Lohagarh Fort (Fig 82).

About twenty-five miles away sits the impressive and beautiful Deeg Palace, built by Suraj Mal, and it was here that Constance lingered longest to paint Suraj Bhawan, one of several attractive pavilions that surrounded the garden. She positioned herself looking out from the interior at the southwest corner of the Mughal-style water garden, but

81   Constance Villiers Stuart, ***The Diwan-i-Khas, Chachrauli Palace***,
1924, watercolour

82   Constance Villiers Stuart, **The Fort, Bharatpure**, 1924,
pencil

with only the merest hint of the walkways, flowerbeds, trees, shrubs and five hundred symmetrically arranged fountains that lay beyond her vantage point. The result was *The Red Door, Suraj Bhawan, Deeg*, in which Constance pays great attention to the architectural details, emphasising inlaid marble decoration of flower forms and geometrical patterns, as well as a large bowl of fruit (Fig 83). According to the Koran, paradise awaits the faithful in a place where 'fruits are within easy reach and just waiting to be enjoyed', where water flows amid shaded groves of tall trees filled with birds, and the scent of flowers wafts across channels of wine, milk and honey. Such essential individual elements were depicted frequently in Mughal paintings and mosaics and had remained of interest to Constance eleven years after the publication of *Gardens of the Great Mughals*, and for decades beyond. On the facing page of her sketchbook, she made individual watercolour drawings of two types of iris motifs, together with a mini-view through a doorway, and a list of flowers growing in the garden at Deeg (Fig 84).

Although the purpose of Constance's trip to Rajputana, meaning 'Land of the Rajputs', (now Rajasthan) is unclear, it is likely she was considering undertaking another project specifically about the Mughal influence on Rajput architecture and gardens. Certainly, the cities which she visited after Deeg – Jaipur, Amer and Udaipur – indicate this; all are famous for their magnificent monumental Rajput forts and palaces. There is just one complete sketch from the last leg of Constance's journey in the region, that of Amber Palace at Amer, near Jaipur, suggesting that sketching time was in short supply during this trip. Constance made fewer watercolours and more pencil drawings than usual and of these, most are scantily rendered and occasionally reduced to mere outlines. *Steps to the Upper Palace* (Fig 85), is a very tiny detail from the vast colossus that is Amber Palace, and the most finished. Undoubtedly, in its massive entirety, the building was a daunting subject, impossible to tackle on a fleeting visit.

83   Constance Villiers Stuart, **The Red Door, Suraj Bhawan, Deeg**, 1924, watercolour

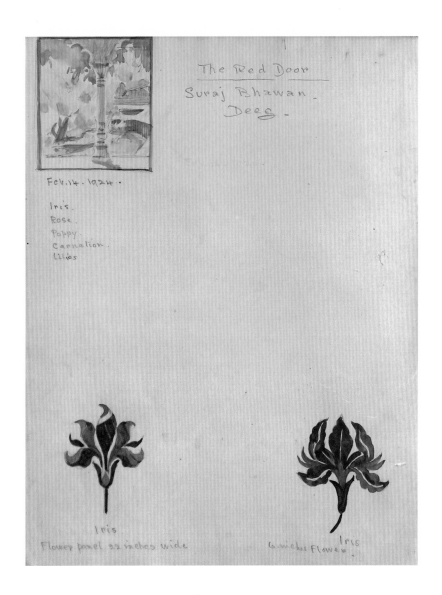

84   Constance Villiers Stuart, sketches, 1924, watercolour

85   Constance Villiers Stuart, ***Steps to the Upper Palace, Amber***, 1924, pencil

Given the time constraints, Constance was more interested in collecting photographs as an expedient way of recalling what she had seen, and she amassed a good set of images, most of them by anonymous photographers. Among these was one of the Queen's *hindola* (swing) at Deeg Palace (Fig 86), an elegant structure reputedly stolen from Agra as a trophy of war by Suraj Mal. The swing had originally been created for the women of the royal entourage so that they could swing out over the fountains to capture the spray and breeze as a means of cooling themselves during the hottest months of the year. This was just the sort of detail that Constance relished. The practical application of the swing, together with the image it provoked in her mind, would have appealed to her hugely, stirring her visual imagination and providing inspiration for a range of possible paintings. Today, although there is an extant seat for the swing, it is used only on rare ceremonial occasions for fear of theft or vandalism. Of the group of photographs Constance collected on this second visit to India, there are a number from Udaipur (Figs 87 and 88) which, along with a local guidebook bearing Constance's name, confirm that she spent time in the city assembling records of architecture for her small but growing picture library.

Constance's use of photographs, not only for reference but also for book and magazine illustration, grew from the 1920s onwards. She had had her own Kodak cameras since the hand-held box camera was introduced in 1888 and, over time, she had become an accomplished photographer. She took most of the photographs for her next book, *Spanish Gardens*, as well as for the numerous magazine articles she wrote from the 1930s onwards. Although her painting practice kept pace, she increasingly made watercolour drawings primarily for private purposes, concentrating her efforts on painting gardens, Beachamwell Hall, landscapes at home and abroad, flower studies and occasional portraits.

Painting and photography had other uses, as well. They provided an effective means of conveying status and enhancing one's public and

86   Priyalall & Company, **The Marble Swing, Deeg** (swing seat missing),
Plate XXXVII, *Gardens of the Great Mughals*, original print created *c.*1900

87   Unknown, *Gardens of the Maids of Honour (Sahelion ki Bari), Udaipur*,
1924, toned silver gelatin print, ©The British Library

88   Unknown, *Lake Pichola, Udaipur*, 1924, toned silver
gelatin print, ©The British Library

private image, pursuits which Constance deployed with skill whenever she was in England. After the war, she needed to build a better bond with Patricia, who had so frequently been left behind while her parents travelled overseas. The relationship between mother and daughter had become distant and strained, so Constance started a form of visual damage limitation. She commissioned expensive celebrity photographers and portrait painters to reinforce the notion of domestic harmony and closeness and, simultaneously, demonstrate the extent of the family's wealth. She began by engaging the artist Mark Milbanke (1875–1927) to paint a formal double portrait of herself and Patricia (Fig 89). Unfortunately, Patrick hated this picture, complaining that it made Constance look 'much too hard', and asked for it to be sent back and improved. Perhaps he had a point. Milbanke could well have caught an exact expression which was anathema to her husband; he had definitely captured a sense of tension between the sitters – the uncomfortable dynamic between estranged parent and child. Just eight years old, Patricia stares directly at the artist with an angelic, distracted, slightly bored expression, while Constance, dressed in elegant grey satin and tulle enlivened by purple carnations in her sash, gazes at her daughter with a look suggesting slight disdain and irritation. Patricia holds a loose bunch of pink and purple carnations which tastefully offset her pink dress and light grey cummerbund. Constance, with her expert knowledge of Indian flower symbolism, knew that carnations represented devotion and motherly love – precisely the message she wished to impart to future viewers.

When Patricia was photographed, aged twelve, at the prestigious studio of society photographer Marcus Adams in Mayfair, Constance had chosen someone whose name was associated with aristocratic and royal children, thus explicitly signalling her own social ambitions for her daughter. In the portrait (Fig 90), Patricia, hair neatly plaited, is looking wistfully over her left shoulder and wearing a dark dress with a white embroidered collar which, all together, enhances the image of the

89   Mark Milbanke, **Portrait of Patricia and Constance Villiers Stuart**, 1918, oil on canvas, private collection

90   Marcus Adams, *Portrait of Patricia Villiers Stuart*,
1922, platinotype, private collection

well-brought up girl that she was. In 1927, in preparation for becoming a debutante and being presented at court, Patricia was formally photographed again – as was her mother, who would naturally be present at the ceremony – at the studio of Vandyk in Buckingham Palace Road. The founder, Carl Vandyk, had photographed many notable people with enormous success, including Queen Victoria, her son, King George V, European monarchs, British prime ministers and American celebrity actors. Carl's son, Hubert, when he eventually took over the studio and expanded it, built on these achievements, surpassing even his father's illustrious client list and, in the process, receiving twenty-two Royal Warrants.

The two Vandyk portraits are very telling and illustrate perfectly the opposing natures of the two women (Figs 91 and 92). Patricia, who allegedly loathed the idea of being a debutante, solemnly regards the bouquet of roses she is holding, and wears her white veil, satin dress and pearls with an air of resignation, even sadness. Her mother, on the other hand, stares coldly into the distance, bearing an expression of intimidating hauteur. A relative who knew Patricia and Constance well described them in terms of opposition:

> Patricia was very much a Villiers Stuart in looks and
> temperament [and] somewhat unconventional by nature.
> [Her] characteristics were gentleness, originality, other-
> worldliness, unusual intelligence, wise innocence, sensitivity
> and sympathy, a real concern for the plight of the down-
> trodden and the suffering … [She had] a refreshing sense
> of humour and the absurd in life, an absolute absence of
> pomposity or taking herself seriously, a spiritual leaning,
> and a gift for creative self-expression, not class-bound,
> honourable. Marriage to a nice, decent country-squire type
> would have bored her and been untrue to her nature.

91   Vandyk Studio, **Portrait of Patricia Villiers Stuart**, 1927,
silver gelatin print, private collection

92   Vandyk Studio, *Portrait of Constance Villiers Stuart*,
1927, silver gelatin print

On the contrary, Constance was pronounced:

> Formidable, imperious, dominating, authoritarian. [She had]
> a will of steel [and was] a caricature of a grande dame, which
> is the way she saw herself, and what she made of herself.
> [She] personified conviction, self-discipline, dedication to
> her aims in life, absolute self-confidence and determination
> – no grey areas, all black and white – and an incredibly
> powerful inner motor and will; perhaps all traits inherited
> from her North Country forefather, the originator of the
> family fortune. No doubt she was honourable, [and] she was
> generous to those she liked and approved of, to those who
> conformed to her standards.

Constance had no qualms about launching Patricia into the marriage market. Under the respectable guise of The Season – during which mothers treated their daughters like products in an exclusive advertising campaign – there was an expectation that young women would find suitable upper-class or aristocratic husbands. In Patricia's case, Constance's preference was for someone from Norfolk so that Beachamwell Hall was assured of being kept in the family. The whole process was expensive; not only the cost of clothes and jewels needed to embellish Patricia's natural good looks, but the dances, balls, luncheons and tea parties that each mother was required to give were a great drain on resources, although this was not a deterrent for Constance. Patricia did not become engaged after her first Season, and was therefore forced to endure two more rounds, which she interspersed with charity work and pursuing her own interests in London and around the country, but, even so, she did not find a fiancé.

Intent on showing Patricia to a wider pool of possible matrimonial candidates, Constance then commissioned Wilfrid de Glehn to paint Patricia's portrait in 1928 (Fig 93). This portrait, with its pink hues,

93   Wilfrid de Glehn, *Portrait of Patricia Villiers Stuart*, 1928,
oil on canvas, private collection

broad sweeping brush strokes and a style reminiscent of John Singer Sargent,[41] was not only attractive but also extremely fashionable. Proof of its popularity came in January 1930 when the portrait featured on the cover of *Women's Journal* and was circulated to a national readership. Later that year Patricia was photographed by Madame Yvonde (Fig 94), an immensely well-respected and creative society photographer who mixed with artists, suffragettes, actors and writers. It is quite possible that, on this occasion, it was Patricia rather than her mother who chose the photographer, because she and Madame Yvonde shared many similar interests, and both moved in artistic circles.

Whilst Patricia's future weighed heavily on Constance's mind in the late 1920s, her energies were also being directed towards researching and writing *Spanish Gardens: Their History, Types and Features*. As with *Gardens of the Great Mughals*, Constance wanted to chart a pioneering course, and proudly declared that 'no book has been published in England on Spanish Gardens, but two dealing with the subject have appeared in America and one in France.'[42] She believed her viewpoint to be entirely different from the three competing authors because her angle was a unique one, that of exploring the relationship of Spanish gardens to gardencraft in the East and West, something she was eminently qualified to do. To fulfil her brief, she spent several months of 1925 and 1926 travelling through Spain, Portugal and the Balearic Islands. Typically, she researched her subject very thoroughly, consulting museum curators and historians, and interviewing the inhabitants of properties still in private ownership. Constance employed her trusted method of producing aides-mémoire by sketching in watercolour and pencil and taking many photographs. Of the sketches that she worked up into finished paintings with which to illustrate her new book, there are just six, in contrast to the sixteen that she had prepared for *Gardens of the Great Mughals*. Conversely, there are seventy-nine photographs of Spanish locations against nine of Indian sites. A new type of illustration

94   Madame Yvonde, *Portrait of Patricia Villiers Stuart*, *c.*1930, silver gelatin print, private collection

was introduced in *Spanish Gardens*: Mrs Ursula Holding was commissioned to make fourteen black and white line drawings from Constance's photographs (Figs 95 and 96), which relieved the monotony of so many monochrome photographs.[43]

Constance focused on the most internationally famous Spanish gardens, especially those in and around Madrid (El Retiro, La Granja, El Escorial, Arunjuez), those of Andalusia (the Alcázars at Seville and Cordova, and the Alhambra and Generalife at Granada), as well as those further afield, including El Laberinto at Horta near Barcelona and Alfabia and Raxa in Majorca. Her watercolours are primarily of La Granja and Generalife but, unlike the numerous and precise representations of landscape and architecture that she made in India, the Spanish watercolour sketches are fewer in number and in a different style. They are much more fluid and vibrant, as if she wished to capture the essence of a place rather than make an exact replica. As a means of getting accurate replication, Constance's camera had by this stage supplanted her paintbrush.

La Granja[44] is situated close to the small town of San Ildefonsa near Segovia, fifty-six miles north of Madrid, and lies at the base of the Sierra de Guadarrama range of mountains amid dense pine forests. It was described by Constance as one of the least known gardens outside Spain, yet, for her, it had enormous attraction because it brought back memories of Nishat Bagh in Kashmir:

> Seeing Spain after India, ... what most struck me was the
> way the older influences had survived the overwhelming
> French invasion. The garden of all others recalled was
> the Nishat Bagh by the Dal Lake in Kashmir. This first
> impression may have been due to the long lines of the
> avenues and the dark-blue mountain background (alike in
> both cases).

95 Ursula Holding, **The Cypress Steps, Raxa**, reproduced from an original drawing taken from a photograph by Constance Villiers Stuart, p. 88, *Spanish Gardens*, 1929

96 Constance Villiers Stuart, **The Cypress Steps, Raxa**, c.1927, lantern slide

There were other aspects of La Granja which showed a strong Eastern influence: the waterfalls, irrigation channels, the way water flowed through a network of runnels outside the palace as well as inside, where it culminated in a dazzling fountain in the dining room.

The palace had formerly been a monastery and had served as a summer residence and hunting ground for the kings of Spain since the fifteenth century. In 1720, Philip V, the first Spanish king of the Bourbon dynasty, purchased the estate and began to construct a magnificent royal residence; he left intact the monks' old *granja* (grange farm), an ancient, tiled courtyard and a Gothic fountain, around which the new building was planned. Philip V commissioned French sculptors René Thierry and Jean Frémin to make twenty-six sculptural fountains, which were designed to astound and entertain visitors. They were created on a mythical theme and named accordingly: Apollo, Neptune, Andromeda, The Fountain of Waterfalls, The Fountain of the Three Graces, The Eight-Fountain Square, The Fountain of the Jungle, The Fountain of the Winds, and so on. These water features became a sensation, and they remain the main highlight of the gardens today, especially The Fountain of Fame which shoots water up to a height of forty metres. Constance photographed many of these fountains, but the photographs have a static, dull quality in complete contrast to the two which she chose to sketch, one titled *Spring at La Granja* (Fig 97)[45] and the other which she merely called *La Granja* (Fig 98). These two sketches burst with vigour, movement and rich colour, evoking sunshine and mountain air, verve and enjoyment; they enliven the page and reveal Constance to be a skilful image-maker who, regrettably, never fully explored the range of her talent.

Two other watercolours on adjacent pages of the same sketchbook are fashioned in a similar vein, one of a fountain and the other of urns upon a wall (Figs 99 and 100). The location is unidentified, but it is most likely to be the Alcázar of Seville. Both drawings were made rapidly on the spot but are all the more effective for being hasty impressions

97   Constance Villiers Stuart, *Spring at La Granja*, 1925, watercolour

98   Constance Villiers Stuart, *La Granja*, 1925, watercolour

99   Constance Villiers Stuart,
untitled, 1925, watercolour

100   Constance Villiers Stuart,
untitled, 1925, watercolour

rather than literal representations. It was here in Andalusia, home to Seville, Cordova and Granada, that Constance's interests in the collision between East and West resonated most forcefully. This was the area in southern Spain that had been the locus of Arab influence and where she could fully explore the melding of European and Moorish gardencraft.

She began at Cordova, the Mecca of the West, recounting the history of the city from the time when it was first conquered by Abd al-Rahman I, whose love of gardens began as a child in Damascus then grew into a grand passion at Cordova. His enthusiasm for exotic plants, flowers and trees was matched by his grandiose ambitions for architecture which reached its zenith when he ordered the construction of the Great Mosque.[46] Over the next three centuries of Arab rule, his descendants created similar expressions of power and wealth by embarking on large-scale building schemes and exquisite landscape projects. Abd al-Rahman III, the fourth Umayyad Emir of Cordova, used his reign to adorn the city with more palaces, Moorish gardens, bridges and mosques, as well as to enlarge the first Emir's already immense Great Mosque. Another of his projects was the caliphate palace, Medina Azahara, high up on the slopes of the Sierra Morena mountains just outside Cordova, bringing in teams of architects and designers from the East to produce plans for its elaborate gardens. It is now a major archaeological site, only a tenth of which has been excavated, but enough to ensure that it received UNESCO World Heritage status in 2018. But however impressive and important the site was, and is, Constance made no drawings of it nor took any photographs there during her visit, as the excavation of the site was still in its early stages, having only started in 1911. She confined herself to making just one small sketch in Cordova, that of the *Patio del Museo* (Fig 101), from which she eventually made a finished painting (Fig 102) that, in turn, became Plate XL in *Spanish Gardens*.

The Alhambra Palace gardens at Granada, particularly the General-ife, gave Constance plenty of scope for painting. She was attracted to the

101   Constance Villiers Stuart, *Patio del Museo*, 1925,
watercolour

102   Constance Villiers Stuart, **Patio del Museo**, 1925, watercolour,
private collection

highlights – the Court of the Canal, the Lotus Fountain and the Apricot Arcade – and little else. Considering the vast size of the palatial grounds, it was a huge task to see everything, let alone select which of the many fascinating details and vistas to record. The gardens of the Alhambra are still among the most well regarded and influential in the world; their combination of practicality and sensuality, finesse and boldness, simplicity and complexity attract more than 2.5 million people every year. Today's numbers would have surprised Constance, but her book and others like it played a significant part in encouraging ever more visitors to experience Spain's glorious gardens.

Her peaceful experience of an uncrowded, tranquil Alhambra allowed her to savour the views and, at leisure, make comparisons with what she had seen in India. In keeping with the rules of paradise gardens, Mughal and Moorish styles shared many components: an elevated site, a distant mountain backdrop providing a stunning skyline, a natural spring cascading through landscaped terraces into pools or lakes below, then channelled into symmetrical canals within enclosures. The canals, with their raised edges lined with picturesque pots of colourful plants or long borders of flowers and small fruit trees, intrigued Constance and appealed to her eye, even more so when they were lined with overarching jets (Fig 103). She described the fountains of the Generalife as illustrating the 'two predominant Oriental types, both based on the lotus'. The shallow basin, set on a flat round base and carved like a lotus in full bloom, is shown in black and white as Plate XVIII in *Spanish Gardens*, but her readership would have had a better understanding of the context had it been published in its original colour form (Fig 104). Constance's sketch of the other type ('derived from the stalk and pointed bud of the lotus'), was made not at Granada but at the Alcázar in Seville (Fig 105) and was reworked as Plate I, *Pavilion of Charles V*, when the book was published.

Spanish Gardens shows Constance's waning use of watercolour as a medium for book illustration but it also shows her evolving as a writer:

103   Constance Villiers Stuart, ***The Lotus Fountain***, 1925,
watercolour sketch

104   Constance Villiers Stuart, *The Lotus Fountain*, c.1925,
lantern slide

105   Constance Villiers Stuart, untitled sketch for **Pavilion of
Charles V, The Alcázar, 1925, watercolour

it is laid out in more clearly defined sections and is better ordered than its predecessor; its prose is less discursive and almost devoid of personal anecdote; it reads more like an objective educational textbook than the intermingling of historical fact and meandering wistfulness that characterised *Gardens of the Great Mughals*. What the two books have in common is a final chapter that brings the reader up to date with recent developments in their respective countries. She used the last chapter of *Gardens of the Great Mughals* to plead for the recognition of India's Mughal past in the construction of New Delhi, specifically in the gardens of Viceroy's House.

The last chapter of *Spanish Gardens* is devoted not to royal palace gardens, but to those important smaller period houses that were then undergoing restoration or transformation, such as the Casa Carmens[47] in the Albaicín quarter of Grenada and the 'sons' (properties) of Majorca. A *carmen* that she particularly liked belonged to the sculptor Señor Don José Acosta, who had designed his own garden mixing Arab and Roman elements, laid out over a number of terraces, to complement his collection of Arab and Roman antiquities. Another was a grander sort of *carmen*, the privately owned Archbishop's Palace at Viznar, the journey to which had entailed an 'adventurous motor run ... to La Zubia, jolting over the hilly by-road to the village'. It was one of the most untouched and authentic eighteenth-century gardens Constance had seen in Spain, with terraces 'planted on old lines, with cypress trees at the corners of the walks and a medley of flowers and fruit trees enclosed within high clipped box hedges ... and a shallow central fountain basin let into the ground [which] was typically Moorish'.

Other recently designed, replanted or restored gardens that Constance had seen outside of Andalusia included the Torre Güell in Barcelona, a notable 'typical Catalan villa' which had belonged to the Conde de Güell before his death in 1918. He had maintained and developed a notable garden ('kept up in its old style with the addition of many beautiful antique busts and statues'), which met with Constance's full approval. The same could not be said of the Parc Güell, a collaboration between Eusebi Güell and his great friend, the modernist architect Antoni Gaudí, for an innovative housing development which began in 1900 and was never completed. Instead, it became Güell's private garden before being converted into a municipal park in 1926 and becoming a much admired and highly regarded tourist attraction and World Heritage Site, renowned throughout the world. But it was not to Constance's taste. Her innate conservatism came to the fore: first, she could not photograph the park successfully and, secondly, she regarded it as incomprehensible, an extraordinary creation of Spanish industrial "new art", and was very perplexed by the 'new forms of Iberian "new art"' that had 'flared up' in Barcelona. However, she was not averse to contemporary advances and showed greater tolerance for the new garden of the Casa del Rey Moro overlooking the Tagus at Ronda, Malaga, which had been designed by the French landscape gardener Jean Claude Forestier in December 1912 and which she rated as 'beautiful' and 'romantic'.

When it was published in May 1929, *Spanish Gardens* was a resounding success and sealed Constance's reputation as a serious, scholarly writer and an artist of merit, adept in both photography and painting. The illustrations were widely praised, and the thoroughness of her research greatly admired. The *Sunday Times* enthused: 'An American author blazed the trail, but this is the first book on the subject by an English writer. May it enjoy the success which such a pioneering book deserves.' Its sentiments were echoed by *Review of Reviews*, which stated: 'Gardeners especially and lovers of the beautiful generally, will delight in this book. Singularly the first English-published book on the subject, and yet the subject is one of entrancing interest.' *Times Literary Supplement* wrote: 'As to the Alhambra, Mrs Villiers Stuart, by treating it as if it were a succession of gardens (as, in effect, it is), has given the best description that has been written for long time.' Academic journals like that of the

Royal Institute of British Architects were similarly impressed: 'Perhaps there is no one who can conjure up like Mrs Villiers Stuart those visions of gardens in Cordova, in Granada, in Agra and Kashmir, where lived and loved the glittering princes of the East and West.' There was international acclaim, too: the *New York Times* described *Spanish Gardens* as '… very beautifully illustrated with over eighty full-page plates, some of them in colour, and with drawings; … [It] is an important and fascinating contribution to a subject of which too little is known by American devotees of the gardening art.'

One critic from *Nation and Atheneum* thought the book would be so influential that it would 'surely infect every reader with a desire to put his English property into the hands of a house-agent and purchase a Balearic "Son".' The book was a triumph and led to numerous interviews, letters of congratulation, a revival of interest in Indian gardens, invitations to write reviews of books and articles about gardens in India and Spain, and to give talks illustrated with slides at various venues, including the Anglo-Spanish Society and the Royal Society of Arts. Constance's reputation was again in the ascendency. She was now highly rated as an expert on Moorish and Mughal gardencraft, and on these subjects, there was no one in Britain to rival her.

Unlike *Gardens of the Great Mughals*, *Spanish Gardens* did not have any agenda to influence future building or landscape projects, as had been the case with Viceroy's House in New Delhi. Not that Constance, with her remarkable tenacity, had given up her hopes of influencing Edwin Lutyens' designs for the viceregal gardens. She tried enlisting influential Indian friends to intervene on her behalf. She approached her friend, the Sultan Jahan Begum of Bhopal, who had been so helpful with the Indian Women's Educational Association, asking her to help find men from the Mistri caste[48] who could be sent to New Delhi to work for Lutyens. Sultan Jahan replied negatively, saying the 'workmen of this country have greatly deteriorated and skilled men are practically unobtainable' and therefore there was nothing she could do to help. This effort was perhaps Constance's last attempt to insert herself into the New Delhi project. In any case, Lutyens had moved on.

Lutyens must have known of Constance's existence – he was likely to have read *Gardens of the Great Mughals* and been receptive to the ideas expressed in it. Lord and Lady Hardinge were strong supporters of Constance, and she had their ear, but Lutyens did not need her advice on the final design of Viceroy's House or on the planting of the Viceroy's Garden, nor did he consult her. For the former, he had his assistants Walter George[49] and, more importantly, Sir Herbert Baker,[50] who was the official partner on the project; for the latter, he turned to the highly knowledgeable and experienced gardener, William Mustoe,[51] whom he described as having the 'genius of an artist'.

After years of discussing whether it should be created in a British or an Indian style, or an amalgam of both, work on Viceroy's House and Garden finally started in 1921. It was agreed that the appropriate style for the garden would be Mughal, and the designs had been approved as early as 1917. Planting did not take place until 1928–1929 and the garden was not officially opened until 1931, when it was hailed as an unparalleled success. It had taken seventeen years to build. Just sixteen years later, in 1947, the Empire would be over and Indian Independence established, making Viceroy's House a very expensive, long-term project which was, ultimately, of short-term benefit to the British. Nevertheless, Constance had been proved right about many aspects of the garden design which, although altered, remains spectacular and admired throughout the world. It has never been definitively verified if her input was even generally acknowledged. Therefore, just how much – or how little – she influenced Edwin Lutyens is a matter of speculation.

CHAPTER EIGHT

Flowers and Finale

Spanish Gardens gave Constance a launching pad for the next stage of her career by cementing her reputation as an authority on historical Indian and Spanish garden design and on horticulture in general. This led to her becoming a more frequent and high-profile contributor to *Country Life* and opened other doors, too: membership of the highly respected Institute of Landscape Architects (now the Landscape Institute), advisory roles in connection with floral design and flower shows, invitations to speak at the Garden Club of America, TV and radio interviews and curatorial involvement in exhibitions of landscape and flower paintings. Yet, despite the increased recognition of her talents, there was, from the 1930s until the end of her life, great personal sadness behind her public persona. The main factors contributing to her anxiety were the deaths of Frances and Patrick, the Second World War, and partial estrangement from Patricia, who had formed a relationship with, and subsequently married against parental wishes, the Yugoslav-Jewish sculptor, Oscar Nemon.

On the professional front, greater affiliation with *Country Life* began through a well-planned promotion of *Spanish Gardens* whereby four excerpts from the book were featured in the magazine in April, June, October and December 1929. Before the first article in the quartet appeared on April 20, Constance invited *Country Life*'s architectural editor, H. Avray Tipping, and the magazine's founder, Edward Hudson, to spend a pleasant spring break at Beachamwell Hall to see her newly designed garden and enjoy her legendary hospitality. Consolidating her relationships at *Country Life* was important because, after 1929, despite her success as an author, she chose not to write any more books. *Country Life* subsequently became the mainstay of her journalism, and she formed a deep and long-lasting friendship with Tipping's successor, Christopher Hussey. He and his wife, Betty, stayed at Beachamwell Hall every August and Constance was a regular visitor at their home, Scotney Castle in Kent. They all shared a passion for gardening as well as architecture; additionally, Constance and Christopher enjoyed painting together in their respective gardens. Beachamwell Hall itself, although not identified, was celebrated in *Country Life* in a feature written by Constance, titled 'The Future of Country House Gardens' (15 March 1946). To enliven the article, she illustrated it with photographs she had taken years before (Figs 106 and 107), but not with any of the paintings she had made of the same view in the 1920s (Fig 108). Unusually, she made several versions of *The Long Walk, Beachamwell Hall,* to test its impact in colour and in black and white; she also used her artistic licence in the watercolour sketch to make the colours of the flowers more dramatic and vibrant.

Besides giving Constance's own garden a stamp of approval, *Country Life* helped to prolong interest in *Spanish Gardens* by drawing on her knowledge into the mid-1930s. This enabled Constance to write at greater length on a single property than had been possible in her book, as was the case in an article for the magazine's 24 October 1934 issue, titled 'The Baroque Garden of Casa Gomis, the Seat of the Marquesa de Gomis.' Interesting though this article is, it is not so much the subject on which Constance wrote but rather the snippets of information she included which provide insight into her changing tastes. We learn that she greatly admires the 'amazing effort and glittering splendour' of Spanish Baroque, which she observes as having filtered down through

106   Constance Villiers Stuart,
The Long Walk, Beachamwell Hall,
undated, Kodak colour print

107   Constance Villiers Stuart,
***The Long Walk, Beachamwell
Hall***, undated, silver gelatin print

108   Constance Villiers Stuart, *The Long Walk,*
Beachamwell Hall, 1926, watercolour

the centuries to the present. In a complete volte-face from the opinion expressed in *Spanish Gardens*, she has, after reflection, come to respect the genius of Antoni Gaudi, acknowledging the debt he owes to the Baroque in his exuberant architecture, in which she sees 'outbursts of the same adventurous Iberian spirit [that has] … inspired the neo-Catalan Temple of Sagrada Familia, that fantastic building which dominates industrial Barcelona with its towers of twisted concrete'.

Constance was a natural journalist, able to interest editors in her (often self-serving) ideas and get their permission to proceed. She was reliable, brought those ideas to fruition and unfailingly delivered copy on time. Within the realms of her remit, she could do mostly what she wanted to do and go wherever she wanted to go. By sheer dogged-ness and seriousness of purpose, she gained access to the best houses and gardens throughout Europe. Whether these were private or state-owned, she ingratiated herself with the custodians, sometimes forming friendships with them by dint of her strong and charming personality and by flattering their vanity with her brilliantly detailed articles and robustly positive descriptions of their properties. Her writing pleased readers, too, and she regularly received responses to her well-illustrated essays, almost always in praise, via the letters pages of various magazines and newspapers. Constance enjoyed the interaction, invariably sending polite and informative replies to her enthusiastic fans.

Journalism did not occupy all of Constance's time. At least up until the Second World War, she continued to paint for enjoyment, frequently choosing flowers as her subject. A series of still-life paintings made at Beachamwell Hall towards the end of the 1920s comprised individual vases containing a specific type of flower. Occasionally, she added a prop such as a book or figurine, for example *Red Star, Lely Colour Scheme* (Fig 109), *Elspeth, French Pastelists 18th Century Colouring* (Fig 110), *Sylvia Slade, Holbein Colouring* (Fig 111), *Donald, French Colouring 20 – Cen* (Fig 112), or *Framfield Red, Rembrandt Colouring* (Fig 113). These

109   Constance Villiers Stuart, **Red Star, Lely Colour Scheme**, 1929, watercolour

110   Constance Villiers Stuart, *Elspeth, French Pastelists 18th Century Colouring*, 1929, watercolour

111   Constance Villiers Stuart, *Sylvia Slade, Holbein Colouring*, 1929, watercolour

112   Constance Villiers Stuart, **Donald, French Colouring
20-Cen**, 1929, watercolour

113   Constance Villiers Stuart, *Framfield Red, Rembrandt Colouring*, 1929, watercolour

sketches were inspired by famous paintings to which Constance wanted to pay homage by using, for her own work, the artists' colour palettes that had already proven to be successful; they also anticipate her later use of colour photography to produce bold and vibrant images of flower arrangements in a variety of ornamental vessels.

Flowers had other connotations for Constance in the 1930s and 1940s, being associated first with the death of her mother and then of Patrick, the two bulwarks of her life. Constance had never lived apart from her mother; they had shared the same living quarters from the time Constance was born until Frances's death, only ever separated when one or the other went abroad. When, after a long illness, Frances died aged eighty-six on 22 November 1936, it was an enormous, almost paralysing blow to Constance, who, sixty years old herself, was completely reliant on Frances's companionship, support and counsel. With such long-standing and intense dependency came a commensurately profound level of grief, softened only by the knowledge that Frances was no longer suffering.

Tributes came in, mostly bearing the same message, that of the sad loss of a benevolent overseer who took a keen interest in the lives of her tenants and the local parishioners. Obituaries reminded readers of Frances's early widowhood and her stoicism in the face of adversity. Few knew of the difficulties she had had in trying to manage the estate after Joshua's death and, indeed, she had persevered through all of them. Her strength was much commented upon: '… she shouldered her responsibilities with a courage and determination which she retained to the last. … After her husband's death she became the capable manager of her large estate (formerly belonging to Sandringham) and the mother of the parish conterminous therewith.' Only two years earlier, in 1934, Frances had celebrated the fiftieth anniversary of moving to Beachamwell from Lancashire by giving a lavish dinner for the staff and tenantry and, in a rare moment of leniency, allowing card games afterwards. Many of those present were children when the Fieldens arrived in 1884 and had grown up in a village which depended for its very existence on the estate, and where tenants' daily lives intertwined with the family in multiple ways.

Although she was compassionate, courteous and upright, Frances was nonetheless a formidable Victorian and practicing Christian with a strict set of moral values; she was not someone who would have been tolerant of the next drama which engulfed her family. Constance herself would have been extremely relieved that Frances did not live to see, first, the deterioration in Patricia's mental health and, secondly, the bitter schism between Patricia and her parents over her lover, Oscar Nemon.[52] From a parental perspective, everything about Oscar was wrong and he could never, under any circumstances, be accepted as a suitable match for their daughter. Patrick, more tolerant, might have mediated the situation, but instead he followed his wife's lead and watched, powerless, as one headstrong woman went into battle with another, equally wilful and determined.

The focus of what became an irreconcilable disagreement was Oscar's obscure background and financially precarious existence. Patricia saw him, as did many others, as a fascinating, romantic-looking, slightly wild, intelligent, artistically gifted, vagabond foreigner possessed of powerful animal magnetism. Her parents saw him in a radically different light, as a penniless, Jewish, womanising, bohemian adventurer and fortune hunter. In reality, Oscar was a talented sculptor and a decent, if erratic, man; he was born in 1906 in Osijek, Croatia, close to the Hungarian border, and as a teenager developed ambitions far beyond his homeland. As soon as he could, he left Croatia to study sculpture in Vienna and Paris before completing his art education at the Académie Royale des Beaux-Arts in Brussels. He had considerable success in Belgium, quickly achieving a solid reputation for his traditional figurative busts of notable sitters. A career-defining moment came in 1931 when Oscar was invited to Vienna and commissioned to make a sculpture of Sigmund Freud, an event which significantly burnished the artist's credibility. More importantly, the two men formed a lasting friendship which, ultimately, led Oscar to a chance meeting with Patricia in London.

Oscar moved to England in the mid-1930s. At the time, a friend and colleague of Sigmund Freud's, Dr Ernest Jones, was running a successful psychoanalytical practice in London and treating a new patient, Patricia Villiers Stuart, for symptoms of mental distress and anxiety. At some point in 1936, Oscar took his letter of introduction from Freud and presented himself to Dr Jones, who was sufficiently intrigued by the compelling young artist to invite him to a party at his home. It was at Ernest Jones' soirée that Patricia and Oscar met and, soon afterwards, began an ardent affair. Constance, when she found out, was appalled: Oscar had no money, no title, no land, no proper home, no reputation – except as a philanderer – and he was Jewish, which, for Constance, was socially unacceptable.

Anti-Semitism had seen a resurgence in Britain between the two world wars, partly fuelled by Oswald Mosley's politics[53] and by a strong pro-German sentiment then embedded in parts of the British Establishment. The Royal Family had strong familial links with Germany, particularly through Queen Victoria – both her mother[54] and her husband, Prince Albert of Saxe-Coburg and Gotha, were German, as was her Governess, Baroness Lehzen, and the language was often spoken at court. In the early years of the twentieth century, it was not uncommon for young aristocratic women to spend a season in Germany to learn the language, attend balls and meet eligible men. Between the wars, some among the British upper classes became Nazi sympathisers, met and were entertained by Adolf Hitler, and held anti-Semitic views. One of their reasons for lending support to Hitler was the belief that Germany was a strong nation with the ability to squash the infiltration of communism from the Soviet Union, something then feared as an imminent threat to British society. Although the rise of anti-Semitism was palpable when Oscar and Patricia met, they themselves were never victims of violence or intimidation, but the prevailing negativity towards Jews in the 1930s and the early years of the Second World War affected them profoundly and made them extremely fearful.

Constance was unremitting in her bigotry towards Oscar, which became more entrenched when he and Patricia moved to Oxford and began living together. Intolerance resolved into hatred when Patricia became pregnant in 1941.[55] The situation obsessed Constance: her hopes and aspirations had been destroyed, she was embarrassed and distraught, and she believed that the future of Beachamwell Hall, the house in which she and Patrick and her parents had invested so much time, money and love, was in great jeopardy. She therefore considered it her right and duty, as a mother, to end her daughter's relationship in order to save her from ruination.

However, Patricia was equally adamant and refused to acquiesce in Constance's rigid, controlling, intractable and hard-hearted behaviour. This domestic strife was developing against a backdrop of war which exacerbated stress in everyone's lives. Frequent air raids, bombardments, blackouts, the devastation of cities such as London, Coventry, Liverpool and Belfast, together with the death of friends and relatives, made people throughout the country hypersensitive, depressed and paranoid. It is likely that the tension and strain of the whole nation greatly intensified the Villiers Stuarts' own heightened emotions. Patricia and Oscar, still only in their thirties, were just trying, in a time of uncertainty and misery, to give expression to how a creative modern couple might live their lives and enjoy a modicum of freedom.

The whole episode shows Constance in a very bad light, as a racially prejudiced, bitter and snobbish woman. Frustrated by Patricia's failure to comply with her wishes, Constance had even resorted to subterfuge in 1937–1939 when she attempted, unsuccessfully, to have Oscar deported to Germany where he would have faced certain imprisonment or death. She remained merciless and without any compassion for her daughter's feelings; she refused to allow Oscar ever to visit Beachamwell – although her grandchildren were welcomed; she kept Patricia on a tightly controlled allowance, and regularly threatened to disinherit her.

Constance simply could not understand how Patricia could settle for a relatively impoverished and insecure life. Why couldn't she be more like her great-grandmother, Sarah Cockcroft, who had used her physical attractiveness to make two advantageous marriages? Constance concluded that beauty and rarity always garnered a high price and, therefore, if Patricia could not recognise her own attributes and capitalise on them then she would no longer support her unconditionally. Instead, she would switch her allegiance back to her work, where she could celebrate loveliness, fragility and transience in a floral world she could control. Patricia never forgave her mother for her autocratic conduct towards Oscar Nemon but, fortunately, over time her attitude towards her father softened, recognising that the 'conflict between his kind hearted nature and mother's fanatical bigotry' meant Constance would always triumph.

During this bleak period from 1936 until the end of the war in 1945, Constance wrote only a few articles, painted infrequently and, owing to wartime restrictions, ceased going abroad. She turned her attention instead to the garden at Beachamwell Hall. With its stunning features, including the Long Walk, a sunken garden, statuary, colourful borders, sprawling lawns and surrounding parkland – all designed by Constance and nurtured by her gardeners – she found solace and an escape from fighting the domestic battles for which she was largely responsible. With the help of her loyal and long-serving Head Gardener, Mr Turner (Fig 114), Constance became increasingly keen on cultivating flowers not merely to have an attractive garden but also to satisfy her growing interest in flower arranging.

There were other signs, too, of a change in direction. Just before the Second World War, in March 1939, Constance had travelled to Portugal

114   Constance Villiers Stuart, Mr Turner, Head
Gardener at Beachamwell Hall, c.1945, silver gelatin
print

and made a series of paintings of native wildflowers (Figs 115–118) similar to but more rapidly executed than the ones she had produced at Beachamwell a decade earlier. Like those, the Portuguese sketches show her artistic impulses veering towards making still-life watercolours of flowers combined with forays into botany. Constance also started to attend exhibitions of Old Master paintings depicting fruit, flowers and landscapes. She became so enamoured of these public displays that she later found ways to curate exhibitions herself and to decorate the galleries with her own floral arrangements in imitation of, or in response to, the pictures she had selected.

As a worshipper of beauty, a quality ubiquitous in the natural world of plants, trees and flowers, Constance understood why, at certain times in history, vast sums had been paid for unusual, exotic species, and great care had been taken to ensure their survival.[56] Constance's own attitude towards plants was thoroughly colonial, exemplified in her perceived entitlement to possess rare examples of flowers, uprooting them and cultivating them far from their native habitats. She had delighted in shipping a consignment of Kashmiri Crown Imperials from India to England; Patrick, too, was proud of the acorns he had collected in Salonica, planted at Beachamwell Hall and seen grow and flourish along its winding driveway.

Plant collecting, managing the Beachamwell Estate and travelling for work and pleasure were just some of the interests which Constance shared with Patrick. He had sketched with her, proofread and edited her books and articles, praised her attainments and indulged her whims. When he died suddenly of a heart attack in the spring of 1949, Constance was effectively left without much love in her life. Lacking siblings, estranged from Patricia and partially so from her grandchildren, with many relatives and friends living far away, life became much lonelier. Patrick was the more popular and sympathetic of the two and, unlike Constance, he was born without the need to always be proving himself

115   Constance Villiers Stuart, *From the Atlantic Cliffs*, 1939,
watercolour and pencil

Casa de Pesça, Deiras.
March 25. 1939.

116   Constance Villiers Stuart, **Casa de Pesça, Deiras**, 1939,
watercolour and pencil

117   Constance Villiers Stuart, **Between Zueluz & Sintra**, 1939, watercolour and pencil

118   Constance Villiers Stuart, **Cintra Foothills and Guincho Beach**, 1939, watercolour and pencil

or controlling others. His background, upbringing, successful military career and his exemplary management of the Beachamwell Estate had given Patrick a strong sense of self-worth.

Obituaries eulogised his achievements during the First World War. He had been a well-liked Brigadier-Major to the 30th Brigade of the Royal Fusiliers at Gallipoli and Salonica, before commanding the 7th Battalion of the Oxford and Buckinghamshire Light Infantry from 1915 to 1916, then being appointed military representative in Bulgaria from 1917 to 1919. Patrick was mentioned in dispatches, awarded the Distinguished Service Order and received a Chevalier of the Legion of Honour.[57] Of his character it was said that 'he had the true Irishman's goodwill and humour, and was one of the old school of landed gentry fast dying out'.

The funeral was attended by many friends and numerous members of the family who watched as Patrick's coffin, draped with the Union Jack upon which had been placed a white-plumed helmet, a regimental sword and his medals, was carried to Beachamwell Church on a horse-drawn farm wagon. The sad event was marred by acrimony between Constance and Patricia, the latter writing afterwards: 'I have so clearly the feeling that my father's spirit hasn't stayed here for a minute more than it need to and has returned to Ireland, the feeling that he could never be a ghost here because he lived here as half a ghost in life.' She continued, noting 'mother's bitterness and aggressiveness to all members of the Villiers Stuart family (it is sugar coated) becomes as it were a charged battery of powerful concentrated mental evil'. Gradually, boiling passions reduced to a steady simmer, and life became marginally less fraught after the war.

Constance periodically reverted to journalism from the mid-1940s until the end of the 1950s, and travelled widely throughout Europe for *Country Life*, describing for its readers the splendours of great European houses and gardens in Germany, Austria, Denmark, Belgium, Sweden, Holland and France. After a long pause, her first article for the magazine appeared in August 1945, shortly before the war officially ended in September, and was indicative of her new direction. Titled 'The British Way of Life: A Lead from Sweden in Museum Display',[58] the opening lines, consciously or not, referred indirectly to her own challenging personal circumstances: 'There are periods in world history when the present is all absorbing. At others the world looks backwards to a golden age or forward to a millennium – or a dark, uncertain future.' The words bear no relation to the body of the article, in which she unfavourably compares London's Victoria and Albert Museum's method of showcasing its collection with Stockholm's Nordiska Museet's 'better ensemble'. She quotes a 'well-known authority' who described the Victoria and Albert Museum as having the 'finest things in the world [and] the worst arranged', and goes on to explain how, whenever the art treasures returned to the museum after being in wartime storage, the deficiency could be rectified by following Sweden's example. It was perhaps galling for the V&A's Director, Sir Leigh Ashton, to read this unsolicited advice, especially as Constance had limited expertise in museum practice and hardly any experience of organising exhibitions.[59] Yet, as seen in previous instances, Constance had enormous confidence in her own opinions, enjoyed using her platform as a journalist to voice them and was always ready to challenge or cajole those in positions of authority to prove her point. There and then, she decided to mount her own exhibition as soon as an opportunity arose, and she would do it in a manner similar to that of the Nordiska Museet.

In September 1946, the Victoria and Albert Museum opened *Britain Can Make It*, an exhibition of contemporary design aimed at boosting the British economy and offering the war-weary nation a vision of a cleaner, sleeker, healthier world. It attracted over 20,000 visitors a day, all eager to see 'today and tomorrow, not yesterday' through consumer goods ranging from cutlery and toys to bathrooms and living rooms. Three months before the opening, Constance proposed to Brenda Colvin,[60] an influential member of the Institute of Landscape Architects (ILA), the idea of adding flowers to the displays, and asked for her help in getting volunteers to create and recreate the arrangements. Brenda answered politely 'most landscape architects would be unable to spare the time to go to the exhibition twice a week to arrange the flowers, attractive though this job might be, … and, unless the scheme is for an indoor room it is not quite a landscape architect's job.' She suggested that the highly fashionable florist and educator Constance Spry be approached instead. Perhaps knowing that this might not be enough to discourage further correspondence, Brenda offered to ask the director of the School of Planning's landscape course whether any of the students would like to do it.

Constance immediately fired back with a barbed response, contradicting Brenda's remarks by writing: 'Having lived so much in India I do not draw a sharp line between house and garden. The decoration of house, garden and park all seem to me the province of the landscape architect.'[61] Constance also refuted the suggestion of asking for Constance Spry's assistance on the basis that 'it would seem a pity if she is thought the only source of flower arrangement, when it is really a national art in England.'[62] To further support her case for having flowers at the V&A, she cited the example of the Fitzwilliam Museum in Cambridge which had, under the directorship of Sir Sydney Cockerell, used 'a panel of architects wives to do the flower arrangements twice a week to suit the pictures and furniture', adding 'and it was lovely.' Constance could not bear not having her own way and it seems she won on this occasion. She succeeded in organising flowers for the Furnished Rooms section of the exhibition, then hammered home her victory by writing to the ILA in November to ask disingenuously whether they had seen her article 'Doing the Flowers for Britain Can Make It' which had been published in *Queen* magazine.[63]

In July 1948, Sir Henry Hake, Director of the National Portrait Gallery, visited Norwich Castle Museum in Norfolk to open a loan exhibition from Norfolk and Suffolk country houses titled *Portraits in the Landscape Park* which he described as 'quite delightful, one of the most charming I have seen. It warms my heart entirely.' The following month, Queen Mary paid an informal visit and declared the show 'very beautiful' before lavishing compliments upon the two organisers – Constance Villiers Stuart and the museum's Curator, Miss G. V. Barnard. Not only had Constance propelled herself into a new cultural realm, but she had also copied precisely the Swedish model she had espoused in *Country Life* three years previously. What Constance had seen at the Nordiska Museet was a series of rooms from different eras, arranged chronologically in settings as they would have appeared in their day, which had inspired her to write: 'Far from being a dry, historical experiment, each room with its beautifully chosen wall decorations, pictures and furniture, is a work of art in itself … [and] tells the country's story.' With her co-curator, Miss Barnard, Constance combined fine furniture from the eighteenth and early nineteenth centuries with contemporaneous paintings, appropriate architectural treatment of wall spaces and magnificent flowers to add an immersive element to the overall aesthetic experience.

The inclusion of flowers was a surprising and welcome bonus; their scent and vivacity soothed and cheered the viewer. Constance had organised a team of flower arrangers, herself at the helm, to create marvellous displays of flowers around the galleries to augment and brighten the exhibits. It was a very popular decision, and one which pleased the public enormously; it was also extravagant in that the arrangements were changed every two days – approximately thirty-nine times over the course of the exhibition. One delighted visitor wrote a letter to the *Eastern Daily Press*: 'Quite apart from the Masterpieces and exquisite old furniture which form one of the finest exhibitions ever held in the Norwich [Castle] Museum, visitors should lose no time in seeing the equally lovely arrangements of flowers placed on antique tables, for unlike the other exhibits, they cannot last.' It was unusual to see so many large bunches of dahlias, roses, gladioli and chrysanthemums blazing among the Gainsboroughs, Hoppners and Romneys. Works had been loaned by many houses, including Raynham Hall, Houghton Hall, Holkham Hall, Hillington Hall, Ickworth House and Euston Hall. The exhibition was well reviewed in the local press, as well as in *The Times* and *Country Life*. Constance wrote the *Country Life* article herself,[64] very effectively promoting her own exhibition.

To stay relevant in post-war Britain, Constance had to rid herself of her elitist and snobbish attitudes (or at least try to conceal them) and adapt to the more egalitarian ideas of a rapidly modernising world. In the professional sphere, this was vital and, as a result, she slowly began to modify her views – at least publicly – to reveal a social conscience. When she wrote about and contributed to other exhibitions, it became important to include an element of benevolence. In the late 1940s, Constance lent a group of photographs of the Long Walk at Beachamwell Hall to the London County Hall, a twentieth-century building still being enlarged up until 1939 and therefore almost a byword for modernity. It was located on the South Bank of the River Thames, which, in itself, represented a departure from the usual exhibition venues. The Long Walk photographs were reproduced in *Landscape Gardens Past and Present*, a double-page spread in the *Illustrated London News*[65] which drew attention to the Walk's 'pastel borders of flowers of rose, grey and mauve with boxwood arches' that reached a peak of perfection every July. This exhibition was significant not only for where it was held but also because it had been organised in conjunction with the International Landscape Conference, with the aim of bringing horticulture into everyday life. Constance was fast coming round to the idea of conveying to those she called 'the common man' the idea of 'horticulture in all its forms from the laying out of vast landscape gardens and parks to the disposition of pots and window boxes on London balconies and the beautifying of bombed sites with parterres.'

Constance's developing awareness of the need for greater social responsibility began when she was elected a Fellow of the ILA on 5 January 1943. Cognisance of the plight of the poor was virtually a prerequisite for membership. She listed three garden design projects on her application form: a formal garden layout and Spring Rock-Garden at Beachamwell Hall, a formal layout and park planning at Cockley Cley Hall, Norfolk, and an Irrigated Water-Garden laid out at Jubbulpore, Central India. These, together with her books and articles about gardens, made her a very suitable applicant, despite not having her own professional practice. She also mentioned Delhi, saying 'perhaps my share in the viceregal garden at Delhi may be taken as one example of concrete work', obliquely referring to the way *Gardens of the Great Mughals* influenced public opinion or to her own influence over Lord and Lady Hardinge in regard to the Viceroy's garden design. Constance had written to Geoffrey Jellicoe[66] to mention other interests in support of her application:

> There is a great interest here[67] in post-war planning and
> building. And I want to help, if possible, to keep the local
> colour and characteristics. ... I think more land should be
> apportioned to each cottage built by the District Council so
> that every family could have an orchard, as they used to, as
> well as their garden.

Town planning was one of Jellicoe's areas of professional expertise and Constance's words were quite likely written in an attempt to ingratiate herself with him, but, beyond that, adequate social housing and good health were topical areas of concern and considered vital to Britain's recovery after the war. Constance was successfully proposed for membership of the Institute by Geoffrey Jellicoe, and seconded by Marjory Allen, Lady Allen of Hurtwood, herself a well-known landscape architect and promoter of child welfare. She is credited with, among other things, highlighting the need for children growing up in post-war high-rise flats to have access to open spaces and playgrounds.

Following the Institute's lead, Constance began attending conferences to debate better ways to recreate London for all levels of society. During a meeting at the Royal Academy, convened to discuss how best to streamline the capital's local government, instigate positive change in land use and provide better housing, Constance made a plea for green spaces and a different approach to city architecture. She suggested that new family flats be built on a plan of a college quadrangle, with a central grass plot in a manner respecting the national leaning for private gardens and open-air spaces: 'London flats, unlike the fortress flats of Vienna, should be approached directly from the street, without entering the quadrangle, leaving the central court undisturbed by any sort of traffic.' Others present were more concerned with allotments, tool sheds, storage spaces, playing fields and making more use of the River Thames for recreation.

In October 1944, Constance opened an exhibition in Lowestoft which was 'designed to stimulate the general public to a deeper interest in housing'. It took the viewer pictorially from mediaeval times to the present and included designs for a possible layout of a post-war housing estate that would be able to accommodate 1,000 people. It was called a 'neighbourhood unit' and prioritised peace and harmony and the safety of children by banning through-traffic. The community development had, besides houses, a shopping centre, a school, a church, a recreational centre and a cinema. In her introductory remarks, Constance revealed that she had recently seen prefabricated houses at the Tate Gallery. She praised their fitted kitchens as a 'wonderful advance' and observed 'If you took [the houses] as a temporary caravan or houseboat they are quite good'. Constance, though well-intentioned, was severely out of touch with the lives of ordinary people and had no real understanding of financial constraints, and still less of poverty. Against all her natural inclinations she was trying to change and learn.

Rural regeneration was more appropriate to Constance's background and knowledge. Writing for the *Eastern Daily Press*, she lambasted town planners for imposing their ideas on local communities without sufficient understanding or knowledge of the countryside and its traditions. Decrying the tendency to work on the principle of 'density per acre', fitting in as many people as possible to a confined space, and 'crowding houses together with gardens of all sorts of ugly shapes as long as they measure the same size', Constance wrote forcefully to oppose the trend. Instead, she advocated reconditioning old buildings, such as labourers' cottages, alongside the construction of new ones so that the skills of small local firms and craftsmen could be employed. In addition, the model of an English village with its village green as the central open space, a requisite pond, stream and some trees had worked well for centuries and did not, according to Constance, need changing, least of all by 'officials coming from towns and industrial areas … [who] cling to town standards and find it difficult to shut the book of rules they know and adapt themselves to the much wider possibilities of landscape planning in villages'. She continued to rail against uniformity of design in rural areas for many years. Writing to the ILA in 1957, she fumed: 'If there's one thing that defeats a designer of council houses and gardens, it is the distance back from the centre of the highway the house must stand. 75 ft is prescribed by our modern planners, most of them more accustomed to semi-industrial than agricultural districts!'

When she was not proselytising for open spaces and more gardens in towns, villages and cities across the country, Constance was enjoying making highly saturated colour photographs of flower arrangements which she created in her Flower Room at Beachamwell Hall. It was partly a commercial exercise – the photographs were reproduced as calendars[68] and booklets[69] – and partly a way of recording the displays she had made and did not want to repeat. For example, those created at home when entertaining guests, those produced for local flower shows and, increasingly, the ones she had made for classes and demonstrations in flower arranging. What Constance described as 'The pleasant English art of doing the flowers' had become a fashionable and enjoyable national pastime, thanks in large part to Mrs Constance Spry, who created wonderful floral extravaganzas for Britain's high society. Throughout the country, clubs and societies were springing up to satisfy a public desire to beautify their surroundings with flowers grown domestically or bought from florists.

Constance was again at the forefront of, and a driving force behind, a developing trend in horticulture and its application to indoor decoration (Fig 119). With unflagging energy – all the more remarkable considering she was in her mid-seventies – she threw herself into promoting what was for some a hobby but for others a new career. Writing in *Country Life* in 1952,[70] she observed that 'interest is now rapidly increasing [and] flower decoration has become a career for girls, and a very pleasant one … with more far more scope for individual taste than an office typewriter'. She also regarded flower arranging as an antidote to the analytical approach of urban development, claiming that 'The curves and accidental shapes of flower groupings become more important as the eye demands relief … from the logical severity of modern architecture.'

Although the flower decoration movement emphasised self-expression, Constance laid down some strict rules: 1) Balance the lighting and colour scheme of a room with the tones and hues of the chosen flowers; 2) Flowers must be at least the height of the vase and a half, and if a bowl, the width and a half, the accent being one way or the other, as in architecture; 3) The highest spray must be placed first; 4) Flowers must have fresh water every day. In an arrangement of arum lilies (Fig 120), Constance adhered to her own instructions regarding height of flowers in relation to that of the vase; she also used the dark background of Beachamwell Hall's drawing room to emphasise the whiteness of the flowers. Arum lilies were particularly attractive to Constance.

119   Unknown, Constance Villiers Stuart arranging flowers,
Peckover House, Wisbech, c.1950, silver gelatin print

120   Constance Villiers Stuart, **White and Green Scheme with Arum Lilies**, c.1955, Kodak Panchro-Royal

Reminiscing in *More Flower Schemes*, she wrote: 'I was enchanted the first time I saw them growing wild at the Cape of Good Hope and again when I came across them flourishing luxuriantly round the water-tanks that irrigate gardens south of Lisbon.' White was also very much in vogue, having been made fashionable by the celebrated interior designer, Syrie Maugham, who had specialised in decorating exclusively in shades of white, particularly in London and Le Touquet.

Lightness of hue married to sophistication of form expressed purity and refinement, which Constance demonstrated in a Japanese-inspired arrangement of pale pink crinum and Japanese anemone leaves set against an off-white wall (Fig 121). She admired Japan's tradition of flower decoration (*ikebana*)[71] with its subtle and delicate composition of line, especially when seen against a flat background with no suggestion of depth. For her, Japanese floral art was 'an intimate expression of national taste' and a good way to gain a better understanding of Japanese history and culture. The ways flowers were used in decorative art and their symbolism had been a major theme in *Gardens of the Great Mughals* and once again, years later, Constance reveals a similar fascination for the depth of meaning in the art of Japanese flower arranging, which had for centuries been a part of religious worship and tea ceremonies. She attempted to recreate some Japanese floral designs, instructed by a French diplomat's wife who had studied the subject, but was informed that it took at least two years of serious learning for a European to grasp all the basic elements. Undaunted, Constance wrote, 'I find it amusing to try out any change. It prevents one getting stereotyped and set in one's ways as to which flowers and vases to use in the home.'

Another way Constance disseminated her knowledge of flower arranging to the general public was through a series of short articles, mainly in the *Eastern Daily Press*, with alliterative titles such as *Autumn Annuals*, *Berries and Birds*, *Concerning Chrysanthemums*, *Daffodils are Difficult* and *The Florist's Flower*, or more prosaic headlines: *House Plants*

121   Constance Villiers Stuart, **Pale Pink Crinum with Japanese Anemone
leaves**, *c.*1955, Kodak Panchro-Royal

as Decoration, *Michaelmas Daisies*, *A Cherry Orchard* and *The Month of Peonies*. These columns were written in a very different way from the in-depth essays she had produced for *Country Life*, the *Edinburgh Review* and other journals. Newspapers provided the opportunity to give practical advice: which flowers were the most long-lasting and appropriate for each season; how to choose the right vessel for a particular group of flora; what were the best arrangements for specific occasions; which colours looked good together and how to mix wild and cultivated plants to good effect. Constance had come to believe that such visual riches were for everyone, whether as a hostess's gift to her assembled guests, an offering to a deity, or for a wedding, funeral, housewarming or children's party. She exhorted her readers not to be afraid of colour and urged them to make bold statements, as she herself had in mixing red and pink geraniums with red monarda (Fig 122).

A late-career modification had worked well for Constance; it was in tune with the times and suitable for her advancing years. Not that she was showing any obvious signs of slowing down in the 1950s. One week might see her showing the Queen Mother around the Sandringham Flower Show (Fig 123); the next might see her on a plane bound for an assignment in Europe or America. In preparation for a foreign trip in 1956, her 80th year, she wrote to Geoffrey Jellicoe to let him know that she had been asked by the Massachusetts Horticultural Society in Boston to present her 'Portuguese and Spanish garden design' lecture. She had also been asked to give a talk at the Art Association of Newport, Rhode Island, where she intended to show coloured slides of gardens and English flower decoration. To help her with this, she asked if the ILA would let her have slides of Dutch flower pictures because she was 'anxious to show how our art derives from old Dutch paintings, just as the American style developed from the Japanese'. Other lectures she was planning included 'English Gardens Open to the Public',[72] 'Watteau in the Baroque Garden' and 'English Flower Arrangement'. New York and

122   Constance Villiers Stuart, *Red and Pink Geraniums with Red Monarda*,
c.1955, Kodak Panchro-Royal

123   Unknown, Constance Villiers Stuart and the Queen Mother
inspecting Entries at the Sandringham Flower Show, 1952, silver
gelatin print

Philadelphia were also on her agenda, not to give public talks but to visit museums and see private collections of paintings. After seeing these cities, she would then travel to the final venue on her lecture tour, the Garden Club of Bermuda.

America exceeded expectations in every way. Audiences gave Constance a tremendous welcome and responded enthusiastically to her lectures. In Boston, she stayed comfortably in 'very nice rooms' at the Somerset Club and was entertained throughout the city at cocktail parties, lunches, dinners, and tours of museums, grand houses and opulent gardens. Among her hosts was Helen Coolidge, the widow of John Gardner Coolidge.[73] Mrs Coolidge asked Constance to lunch at 171 Commonwealth Avenue and gave her guest a tour of her spacious home, which had been luxuriously and beautifully decorated with fine Genovese silk embroidery wall hangings and some unusual yellow glassware. Constance was quite overawed by the size and lavishness of this and other houses she visited further along Commonwealth Avenue and in Pinckney, Marlborough, Boylston and Beacon Streets, as well as in Chestnut Hill just outside the city. She was impressed by the paintings, furniture and 'the Victorian manners' of the 'pleasant, interesting and charming' people, among whom she noted a Mr Richard Hobart, whose family had built Blickling Hall, Norfolk, in the seventeenth century. Later in the day following the lunch at Mrs Coolidge's, Constance had delivered her first lecture to 'a good and attentive audience'. Unfortunately, the talk was considered too short: whereas Constance had allowed time for questions within the hour allotted, the Chairman had assumed she would speak for longer. She wrote afterwards with evident surprise: 'most lectures here are an hour!'

After lecturing in Newport, Rhode Island, Constance proceeded by train to Philadelphia where she admired Mount Pleasant House, an eighteenth-century mansion ('small with great dignity') overlooking the Schuylkill River. Most especially, she liked the Du Pont Gardens at

Willington (now Longwood Gardens), where she saw 'a wonderful greenhouse arrangement' and the 'particularly lovely house with tree ferns and cymbidium orchids grown in tubs on the largest scale'. Constance left Philadelphia for New York to spend a few days at the Metropolitan Museum of Art (now The Met), but she found the city too oppressive and hectic 'like the business parts of the London City [district]' and was pleased to fly to Bermuda and give the final lecture of her six-week tour.

In Bermuda, Constance stayed at Government House, which at that time was the home of her cousin, Lady Woodall, who was married to the Governor, Lt. Gen. Sir John Woodall.[74] Bermuda was warm and relaxing, very social and with a schedule that allowed plenty of time for photography, giving interviews, watching tennis at the Coral Beach Club, shopping and going sailing. Constance gave her lecture to the Garden Club of Bermuda at the Agricultural Station and rhapsodised about the abundance of Easter Lilies. These elegant flowers were introduced to the island from Japan in the middle of the nineteenth century and flourished there from January to June, eventually making Bermuda the centre of the American lily market, a position which declined drastically during the twentieth century. Now the famous Easter lily is grown commercially only for domestic use.[75]

Constance's promotion of flower arranging and flower shows, both abroad and at home, was timely and effective. In *Modern Trends in Flower Decoration*,[76] she proudly described how the activity had burgeoned in the past decade:

> A few years ago there was only a small number of flower-decoration clubs … some in Dorset, … one in the Midlands, one in Suffolk, one in Essex and two in Norfolk. Now there are over 400 up and down the country, and the Festival of Flower Decoration held in July, this year by the Royal Horticultural Society filled two large Westminster Halls.

Seemingly tireless, Constance made one final long-distance tour in 1957 to St Petersburg, Russia. Her itinerary was short but intense: Peterhof Palace, the Hermitage, Pavlovsk Palace, Kazan Cathedral and Catherine Palace. The journey was undertaken for a *Country Life* article, 'Peterhof: The Russian Versailles', but, knowing she was unlikely at her age to see Russia again, she saw as much as anyone possibly could in the space of a week. The architecture and gardens were incredible and magnificent, but Constance found the people occasionally infuriating – complaining that 'like India, it's very difficult to get direct answers to any question' – and gloomy: 'the only time I saw them smile was when they were with children'.

Going to Russia at the age of 81 brought Constance back into the public eye for one last hurrah. Lisa Moynihan from the *Evening Standard* was sent to Beachamwell Hall to interview her and hailed her as one of the oldest people ever to apply for a visa. It had been granted just one day before she was due to sail on the SS *Molotov* and, in her haste to leave, she had forgotten to pack warm clothes, perhaps a sign that she needed to rein back her travelling and other activities. The reporter noted her imperiousness when their interview was interrupted by a telephone call from a producer from the BBC, inviting her to the Lime Grove Studios for a TV appearance. Moynihan wrote: 'I hope she makes it. If she does, one thing is certain. The Lime Grove gardening experts will have to look to their laurels.'

Whereas the 1950s were packed with activity, the 1960s were almost devoid of it. There was a marked decline in Constance's output as her health began to deteriorate. Although still involved at times with the ILA, regional flower shows and photographing her flower arrangements, she had begun to complain of frequent colds, sore throats and other minor illnesses, and of falls and broken bones. Showing great fortitude, she was still planning another book and said in a letter written in September 1960 to one of her granddaughters: 'I haven't got round to my book yet.[77] Christmas to Easter is my writing time.' A few months later, she wrote again while ill in bed and forbidden to speak because of 'bad laryngitis'. This could have been an early symptom of the oral cancer which afflicted her final years. For someone so accustomed to public speaking and voicing her opinions as she was, it must have been a terrible setback. In August 1962, Patricia wrote to Oscar Nemon announcing that her mother had been in hospital for several weeks and that they must face the fact that she was dying. But Constance did not die. Tenacious to the end, she lived on for another four years. Constance died at home in her own bed on 6 February 1966, prompting outpourings of praise in obituaries for all her many achievements, and sparing her the pain of seeing Beachamwell Hall and its contents sold in 1967.

At Constance's funeral, the congregation sang *All Things Bright and Beautiful*. It was a well-chosen hymn, as some of the verses, though written more than a century before, seemed tailor-made, almost as if they had been composed with Constance and her Kashmir idyll in mind. Even the pretty, sentimental lyrics venerating birds, mountains, rivers, sunsets and 'all creatures great and small' are reminiscent of certain traits in her own style of writing and bring to mind her abiding love of nature. The natural world, especially when tamed and beautified by human intervention, was a genuine passion that fuelled the finest of Constance's triumphs and accomplishments; it brought out the very best in her and inspired great bursts of creativity, the results of which remain her enduring legacy.

Constance is buried alongside her parents and husband at St Mary's Church, Beachamwell, where she was taken every Sunday as a child and continued to worship throughout her life. During the entire period of her residence at Beachamwell Hall, the church was central to village life, a focus of assembly for the young and old and rich and poor whose families had resided in the area for generations. The 1,000-year-old church, with its memorial plaques – one of which commemorates the

Fielden and Villiers Stuart families – stained glass windows, traditional thatched roof, and rare round tower meant a great deal to Frances and Constance, having pride of place in the midst of their estate. It would have been an immense sadness for them to know that the church burnt to the ground in February 2022, after a fire was accidentally started while repairs to the roof were being carried out. One thing is certain: Constance would have wasted no time at all in spearheading a fundraising campaign for its restoration, and she would not have rested until she had seen the project through to a successful conclusion.

NOTES

1 Now the University of Strathclyde.

2 The Pont-Aven School is a term applied to artists who spent extended periods of time painting in the area, of whom the most well-known are Paul Gauguin and Paul Sérusier. It began in the 1850s and remained active as a loosely connected group until the early twentieth century.

3 The hotel was destroyed by a bomb in the Second World War; the site is now occupied by Nos 25–27 Knightsbridge.

4 Patrick's father, Henry Villiers Stuart (1827–1895), had inculcated in all his children a love of history. He was a recognised traveller and author who wrote extensively about South America and Egypt.

5 Constance defined a *bagh* as 'an enclosed garden' or a 'country-house'. The same word is also used in Persian.

6 Gardeners.

7 A *chabutra* is a raised platform for sitting on.

8 Reproduced as Plate XIX, *Gardens of the Great Mughals*.

9 The Taj Mahal is the mausoleum of Mumtaz Mahal, the wife of Emperor Shah Jahan (r. 1628–58). He commissioned it in 1632 to commemorate his favourite wife.

10 The Lord High Treasurer or Pillar of the State.

11 The coronation took place on 22 June 1911.

12 Marquees.

13 These had been laid by hundreds of Indian gardeners, squatting in long rows and sowing blades of grass on levelled wasteland for months before the lawns grew to perfection after the monsoon season.

14 It is possible that some of Constance's sketchbooks have been lost or destroyed, because there are no sketches of Delhi, and it seems highly unlikely that she could have resisted painting the city's Mughal buildings and gardens, which she so obviously admired.

15 Brigadier-General Sir Percy Molesworth Sykes (1867–1945) was a soldier, diplomat and historian who wrote extensively about Persia.

16 The gondola of Kashmir.

17 Wular Lake is one of the largest freshwater lakes in Asia, stretching twelve miles south to north from Sopore to Bandipora and almost as much from west to east.

18 Literally 'the path to something', *pradakshina* is the practice of clockwise circumambulation of a sacred object or place while in a state of meditation.

19 The Maharaja of Patiala, Bhupinder Singh (1891–1938), married five times and had numerous lovers, reputedly fathering 88 children.

20 Approximately £37 today.

21 Gertrude Jekyll (1843–1932) was a horticulturalist, garden designer, artist and writer who frequently partnered with Edwin Lutyens on architectural and garden projects. Jekyll had already written a book titled *Wall and Water Gardens* in 1902, and between 1904 and 1908 she and Lutyens had designed the layout and planting of the gardens at Hestercombe House in Somerset. These include geometric panels and a water garden which were a departure from the more naturalistic styles popular at the time.

22 See *First Garden of the Republic: Nature in the President's Estate*, Amita Baviskar (Ed), Publications Division, Government of India, 2016.

23 An officer's servant was sometimes referred to as his 'batman'.

24 Then part of the Kingdom of Serbia, now in north Macedonia.

25 Patrick was annoyed at having to abandon his belongings and later wrote: 'A Bulgar staff officer no doubt now sleeps in my flea bag, keeps himself warm in my greatcoat and shares my razor and probably makes his coffee on the Tommy's cooker.'

26 Patrick's was prescient because the Great Thessaloniki Fire of 1917 destroyed two-thirds of the town and left thousands of people homeless.

27 Rear Admiral Hubert Searle Cardale (1875–1940), Head of the British Naval Mission in Greece.

28 Head of the Military Police.

29 At the time, Salonica's population was 39% Jewish, 29% Turkish, 25% Greek, 4% Bulgarian, 2% Roma and 1% other. Many

languages were spoken, including Judeo-Spanish, a dialect of Spanish spoken by the city's Jewish population, and many religions practiced, including Orthodox Christianity, Islam and Judaism.

30 The outer wall was demolished in 1917.

31 In a letter to her mother, Constance mentioned that she was the only British woman in Salonica who was not working in a hospital.

32 Literally 'hairy ones', a term of endearment given to French infantrymen. The term had connotations of being rustic, down-to-earth, dogged, brave and patriotic, an image exploited for propaganda.

33 Approximately equivalent of £17.70.

34 Constance spent the winters of 1925 and 1926 in Spain and said she always wore black because 'if you wear colours, you are either a tourist or a gipsy and everyone makes for you from afar'.

35 According to census records, the total number of people with English as their mother tongue in India in 1891 was 238,409. In 1921, 165,485 British people were resident in India, and in 1947, this number had risen to 800,000, but it diminished rapidly after Indian Independence.

36 Lady Willingdon (1875–1960), Marie Adelaide Freeman-Thomas (née Brassey), Marchioness of Willingdon. Known for her enthusiastic and energic good works in support of health and education, but also for her mania for naming things after herself. Buildings, organisations, streets, parks, gardens and memorials in Australia and India bore the name Willingdon, some of which have now been renamed. She was also renowned for spotting things she liked on official visits and asking for them to be given to her, so much so that on one such visit to Baroda, the state jewels were hidden before her arrival.

37 From 1931 to 1936.

38 Later the National Union of Societies for Equal Citizenship.

39 He served briefly as Acting Viceroy of India in 1926.

40 There are Muslim, Hindu and Sikh Jats, but the Hindu Jat Kingdom of Bharatpur gained prominence in the eighteenth century when Maharaja Suraj Mal (1707–1763) captured Agra from its Mughal rulers. During that era, the Kingdom of Bharatpur reached its apex and covered a vast area but, over time, territory was regained by the Mughals.

Of particular interest to Constance for its Mughal-influenced garden was Deeg Palace, built by Suraj Mal in 1771.

41 Wilfrid G. de Glehn (1870–1951) was known as a British Impressionist. As a young student he attended the Royal Academy Schools in London and the École des Beaux-Arts in Paris. He became an assistant to John Singer Sargent and subsequently formed a lifelong friendship with him. De Glehn had a successful career, exhibiting regularly at the Leicester Galleries and the Royal Academy in London and at overseas venues. He was much sought after as a portraitist and for his paintings of landscapes, cityscapes and marine subjects.

42 M. and A. Byne, *Spanish Gardens and Patios*, New York, 1924; Rose Standish Nichols, *Spanish and Portuguese Gardens*, Boston, 1924; Georges Gromont, *Jardins d'Espagne*, Paris, 1926.

43 The majority of Constance's Spanish photographs were colour glass slides which were reproduced in black and white when *Spanish Gardens* was published.

44 The building's full title is The Royal Palace of La Granja de San Ildefonsa.

45 Reproduced as Plate LXVII in *Spanish Gardens*.

46 Now known as the Mosque-Cathedral of Cordova.

47 Town houses with gardens planted with grapevines, fruit trees and flowers, designed to be an amalgam of kitchen garden and ornamental garden, providing produce, colour, scent, shade and privacy. High surrounding walls ensured that the inhabitants were not visible from the street. They often featured fountains, ponds and water channels.

48 Supervisor or contractor.

49 Walter Sykes George (1881–1962) was a modernist architect who had trained at the Royal College of Art in London before working for Herbert Baker and Edwin Lutyens on the design of New Delhi. He remained in India after the completion of the project in 1931, until his death in 1962.

50 Sir Herbert Baker (1862–1946) was a successful English architect. He and Sir Edwin Lutyens (1869–1944) met while training at the architectural practice of Ernest George and Harold Peto where they became good friends. When Lutyens was given the contract to design New Delhi, he invited Baker to share the commission with him. Unfortunately, over the course of the project, their friendship faltered.

51 William Robert Mustoe (1878–1942) trained at the Royal Botanic Gardens, Kew, and later was a trainee at the Bombay Municipal Gardens before going on to work at the Royal Botanic Gardens, Calcutta, and Government Gardens, Lahore. He was a tree expert who was hired to work on the New Delhi project. Lutyens and Mustoe worked very closely together on the planting of the Viceroy's Gardens, for which Mustoe was awarded the OBE in 1930.

52 Oscar Nemon (1906–1985), originally Oskar Neumann. A Croatian-born sculptor who began his career in continental Europe before moving to Britain in 1936. He developed a successful practice in London, and among his well-known sitters were HM the Queen, HM the Queen Mother, Sir Winston Churchill, King Peter of Yugoslavia, Harold Macmillan PM, and many politicians, musicians and actors.

53 Sir Oswald Mosley (1896–1980) was a British MP who later became the Leader of the British Union of Fascists, famed for forming a defence force of paramilitary stewards called 'Blackshirts'. Mosley was a supporter of Mussolini and Hitler, an anti-Semite and a Holocaust denier.

54 Princess Victoria of Saxe-Coburg-Saalfeld (1786–1861).

55 Patricia and Oscar had three children: Falcon (b. 1941), Aurelia (b. 1943) and Electra (b. 1950).

56 In the seventeenth century, large sums of money were paid for tulips, which became status symbols for rich Dutch merchants. In the nineteenth century, Britain searched for ways to cultivate the water lily and also experienced 'orchid-mania' as garden enthusiasts clamoured for new and rare species. Ships were adapted to ensure safe passage from distant countries and the development of glasshouses meant that fewer species perished on the journey or during transplantation. Plant collecting was a hobby for the wealthy, and an investment for speculators.

57 Even with such an excellent array of awards, there were relatives who remarked wryly that Patrick's biggest act of bravery had been in marrying Constance.

58 *Country Life*, 3 August 1945.

59 Constance had organised an exhibition called *Indian Art from the Ajanta Period to the Present Day* in collaboration with Mr Lawrence Binyon, a poet and Keeper of Prints and Drawings at the British Museum. It was held at the British Indian Union in Grosvenor Square, London, in the summer of 1929. Constance lent the exhibition some Indian paintings from her collection.

60 Brenda Colvin (1897–1961) was a British landscape architect, who co-founded the Institute of Landscape Architects and became its President in 1951.

61 Brenda Colvin was born in Simla (Shimla) and spent her youth there, and her family had lived and served in India for decades. Considering that Constance had spent only two and a half years in India, her reply seems unjustifiably condescending.

62 Perhaps a sign of professional rivalry because Constance had at this stage begun teaching flower arranging in Norfolk.

63 30 October 1946.

64 *Portraits in the Landscape Park: Paintings from Norfolk and Suffolk Country Houses*, 16 July 1948.

65 24 July 1948.

66 Sir Geoffrey Jellicoe (1900–1996) was an architect, garden designer, garden historian and landscape architect. He was a founding member of the Institute of Landscape Architects when it opened in 1929. He was its President from 1939 to 1949.

67 Presumably Norfolk, from where she was writing.

68 *Flower Studies* produced annually, published by Jarrolds of Norwich.

69 *Flower Schemes* (1953) and *More Flower Schemes* (1955), published by Jarrolds of Norwich.

70 28 March 1952.

71 *Ikebana* means 'making flowers alive'.

72 Constance had prepared this lecture to encourage Americans 'to bring some dollars here in the following years'.

73 John Gardner Coolidge (1863–1936) was a US diplomat who had served in France, China, Mexico and Nicaragua. He was from what was known as a Boston Brahmin family (i.e., the elite of American society). His aunt was Isabella Stewart Gardner, who founded the museum of the same name in Boston.

74 Governor of Bermuda from 1955 to 1959.

75 With some exceptions – every year, Buckingham Palace receives bouquets of the lilies as an Easter gift for the Queen from the people of Bermuda.

76 *Country Life*, 17 September 1959.

77 The book was never written.

BIBLIOGRAPHY

Alfrey, N., Daniels, S. and Postle, M. (eds.) (2004) *Art of the Garden*. London: Tate Publishing.

Amherst, A. (1895) *A History of Gardening in England*. London: Bernard Quaritch.

Anand, A. (2015) *Sophia: Princess, Suffragette, Revolutionary*. London: Bloomsbury.

Bachelard, G. (1969) *The Poetics of Space*. (1994 edition). Boston: Beacon Press/Grossman Publishers.

Baddeley, M. J. B. (1880) *Thorough Guide to the English Lake District*. London: Dulau & Co.

Barr, P. (1976) *The Memsahibs: The Women of Victorian India*. London: Secker and Warburg.

Barr, P. (1989) *The Dust in the Balance: British Women in India 1905–1947*. London: Hamish Hamilton.

Baviskar, A. (2016) *First Garden of the Republic: Nature in the President's Estate*. New Delhi: Publications Division, Government of India.

Beckert, S. (2014) *Empire of Cotton: A New History of Global Capitalism*. London: Allen Lane.

Bénézit, E. (1960) *Dictionaire Critique et Documentaire des Peintres, Sculpteurs, Dessinateurs et Graveurs*. (Tome huitième, Soane – Z.) Paris: Librairie Gründ.

Bennet, J. H. (1870) *Winter and Spring on the Shores of the Mediterranean*. (Fourth edition). London: John Churchill & Sons.

Blomfield, R. (1892) *The Formal Garden in England*. London: Macmillan & Co.

Bowe, P. (2009) 'The Genius of an Artist: William R Mustoe and the Planting of the City of New Delhi and its Gardens', *Garden History*, 37(Summer 2009), pp. 68–79.

Brabant, F. G. (1905) The English Lakes. London: Methuen & Co.

Bradley, J. (ed.) (1986) *Lady Curzon's India: Letters of a Vicereine*. American edition. New York: Beaufort Books.

Brendon, P. (2007) *The Decline and Fall of the British Empire 1781–1997*. London: Jonathan Cape.

Brendon, V. (2005) *Children of the Raj*. London: Phoenix.

Bryant, J. and Weber, S. (eds.) (2017) *John Lockwood Kipling: Arts and Crafts in the Punjab and London*. New Haven and London: New York & Yale University Press, Bard Graduate Center Gallery.

Cannadine, D. (2001) *Ornamentalism: How the British saw their Empire*. London: Allen Lane.

Clark, E. (2004) *The Art of the Islamic Garden*. UK: The Crowood Press Ltd.

Cox, H. (ed.) (1928) *The Edinburgh Review*. Edinburgh: Longmans.

Douglas-Home, J. (2011) *A Glimpse of Empire*. Norwich: Michael Russell Ltd.

Duke, J. (1910) *Kashmir and Jammu: A Guide for Visitors*. Calcutta and Simla: Thacker, Spink & Co.

Gailey, A. (2016) *The Lost Imperialist: Lord Dufferin, Memory and Mythmaking in an Age of Celebrity*. London: John Murray.

Gascoigne, B. (1998) *A Brief History of the Great Moghuls: India's most Flamboyant Rulers*. London: Constable & Robinson Ltd.

Gerrish, H. (2011) *Edwardian Country Life: The Story of H. Avray Tipping*. London: Frances Lincoln Publishers.

Hardinge, C. (1947) *Old Diplomacy*. London: John Murray.

Hardinge, C. (1948) *My Indian Years 1910–1916: The reminiscences of Lord [Charles] Hardinge of Penshurst*. London: John Murray.

Hayward, A. (2007) *Norah Lindsay: The Life and Art of a Garden Designer*. London: Frances Lincoln Publishers.

Herbert, E. W. (2011) *Flora's Empire: British Gardens in India*. Philadelphia: University of Pennsylvania Press.

Hussey, C. (1953) *The Life of Sir Edwin Lutyens*. London: Country Life Ltd; New York: Charles Scribner's Sons.

Jekyll, G. (1902) *Wall and Water Gardens*. London: The Country Life Library.

John Murray (Firm). (1870) *Handbook for Shropshire, Cheshire and Lancashire*. London: John Murray.

Law, B. R. (1995) *Fieldens of Todmorden: A Nineteenth Century Business Dynasty*. Lancashire: George Kelsall.

MacKenzie, J. M. (1995) *Orientalism: History, Theory and the Arts*. Manchester and New York: Manchester University Press.

MacKenzie, T. M. (1907) *Dromana: The Memoirs of an Irish Family*. Dublin: Sealy, Bryers & Walker.

Macmillan, M. (1988) Women of the Raj. London: Thames and Hudson.

Mathur, S. (2007) *India by Design: Colonial History and Cultural Display*. Berkeley and Los Angeles: University of California Press Ltd.

Matless, D. (1998) *Landscape and Englishness*. (Revised 2016). London: Reaktion Books.

Millar, D. (1996) *Watercolours of Charlotte, Viscountess Canning, Lady in Waiting to Queen Victoria*. UK: Harewood.

Minter, S. (2010) *The Well-Connected Gardener: A Biography of Alicia Amherst, Founder of Garden History*. Brighton: Book Guild Publishing.

Moynihan, E. B. (1979) *Paradise as a Garden in Persia and Mughal India*. (1982 edition). London: Scolar Press.

Nicolson, N. (1977) *Mary Curzon: A Biography*. (1998 paperback). London: Phoenix Giant/Orion Books Ltd.

Pavlović, N. (2021) 'Review of the book titled "Great Women in the Great War"', Srp Arh Celok Lek, 149 (7–8), pp. 516–517.

Payne, M. (2011) *Marianne North: A Very Intrepid Painter*. London: Royal Botanic Gardens/Kew Publishing.

Percy, C. and Ridley, J. (eds.) (1985) *The Letters of Edwin Lutyens to his Wife Lady Emily*. London: William Collins Sons & Co.

Prior, M. A. (2018) 'An Impulse of Genius', *Country Life*, CCXII(37, 12 September), pp. 100–104.

Rasmussen, S. E. *et al.* (1992) *Karen Blixen's Flowers: Nature and Art at Rungstedlund*. Copenhagen: Christian Eilers Publishers.

Shephard, S. (2010) *The Surprising Life of Constance Spry*. London: Pan Books.

Sinha, S. (1947) *Kashmir: The Playground of Asia, A Handbook for Visitors to 'the Happy Valley'*. Allahabad: Ram Narain Lal.

Sitwell, G. (1909) *On the Making of Gardens*. (2003 edition). Boston: David R. Godine.

Sloan, K. (ed.) (2017) *Places of the Mind: British Watercolour Landscapes 1850–1950*. London: The British Museum/Thames & Hudson.

Superintendent Government Printing (1911) *Coronation Durbar Delhi 1911: Official Directory with Maps*. Calcutta: Superintendent Government Printing.

Tinniswood, A. (2016) *The Long Weekend: Life in the English Country House 1918–1939*. New York: Basic Books (Perseus Books Group).

Villiers Stuart, C. M. (1913) *Gardens of the Great Mughals*. London: Adam and Charles Black.

Villiers Stuart, C. M. (1914) 'In the Garden: An Indian Garden Book', *Country Life*, XXXV(888, 10 January), pp. 53–54.

Villiers Stuart, C. M. (1915) 'Indian Garden Palaces', *Country Life*, XXXVII(962, 12 June), pp. 827–832.

Villiers Stuart, C. M. (1916) 'Rajput Pastorals', *Country Life*, (15 April), pp. 8–10.

Villiers Stuart, C. M. (1916) 'Photographed from an Aeroplane: Soldiers Gardens around Salonica', *Country Life*, XL(1022, 5 August), pp. 145–148.

Villiers Stuart, C. M. (1916) 'Three Kashmir Flowers', *Country Life*, XL(1024, 19 August), pp. 201–203.

Villiers Stuart, C. M. (1929) *Spanish Gardens: Their History, Types and Features*. London: B. T. Batsford Ltd.

Villiers Stuart, C. M. (1929) 'The Gardens of Spain: El Laberinto, Barcelona', *Country Life*, LXV(1683, 20 April), pp. 554–560.

Villiers Stuart, C. M. (1929) 'Spanish Mediterranean Gardens: Raxa, Majorca', *Country Life*, (1 June), pp. 776–778.

Villiers Stuart, C. M. (1929) 'Spanish Mediterranean Gardens: Some Gardens in Majorca', *Country Life*, LXVI(1708, 12 October), pp. 482–485.

Villiers Stuart, C. M. (1929) 'The Gardens of Spain: The Garden Palace of La Granja', *Country Life*, LXVI(1719, 28 December), pp. 931–935.

Villiers Stuart, C. M. (1931) 'Persian Gardens and Persian Art', *Country Life*, (21 February).

Villiers Stuart, C. M. (1934) 'A Baroque Garden at Barcelona: Casa Gomis, the Seat of the Marquesa de Gomis', *Country Life*. LXXVI(1970, 20 October), pp. 424–426.

Villiers Stuart, C. M. (1945) 'A British Way of Life: A Lead from Sweden in Museum Display', *Country Life*, XCVIII(2533, 3 August), pp. 194–196.

Villiers Stuart, C. M. (1946) 'The Future of Country House Gardens', *Country Life*, XCIX(2565, 15 March), pp. 490–491.

Villiers Stuart, C. M. (1948) 'Portraits in the Landscape Park: Paintings from Norfolk and Suffolk Country Houses', *Country Life*, CIV(2687, 16 July), pp. 124–125.

Villiers Stuart, C. M. (1952) 'Doing the Flowers', *Country Life*, CXI(2880, 28 March), pp. 912–913.

Villiers Stuart, C. M. (1959) 'Modern Trends in Flower Decoration', *Country Life*, (17 September).

Wilton, A. and Lyles, A. (1993) *British Watercolours 1750–1880*. London and New York: Prestel.

Young, A. and Hale, J. (2018) *Finding Nemon*. London: Peter Owen.

INDEX

Page numbers in **bold** refer to
  illustrations

A & C Black, 132, 134, 163
Abd al-Rahman I and III, 195
Aberdeen Journal, 102
Académie Royale des Beaux-Arts, Brussels,
  217
Achibal (Achabal) gardens, 93–94,
  99–100
Acosta, Señor Don José, 202
Adams, Marcus, 179
Adelaide, 46
Agra, 102–109
Agra from the Taj (1911, watercolour),
  107–108
Akbar's tomb, Sikandra, 104
Alagoa Bay (South Africa), 46
Albaicín quarter, Granada, 202
Albert, Prince, 218
Alcázar, Cordova, 189
Alcázar, Seville, 189, 191, **194**, 198
Alexandra Hotel, 73
Alfabia, Majorca, 189
Alhambra, Granada, 189, 195, 198, 203
Allen, Marjory, Lady Allen of Hurtwood,
  232
Amber Palace, Amer, 171, **175**
Amherst, Alicia (Mrs Evelyn Cecil), 58,
  138
Anantnag, 93
Anglo-Spanish Society, 204
anti-semitism, 218
Arab Women, Port Said (unknown), **39**
Arch of Galerius, Salonica, 155
Archaeological Survey of India, 109
Arkwright, Sir Richard, 19
Art Association of Newport, Rhode
  Island, 240
Arum lilies, 235–238
Arunjuez, 189
Ashtadhatu Gate, Bharatpur, 168
Ashton, Sir Leigh, 228
Athens, 146

Aurangzeb, Emperor, 101
*Autumn at Achibal, Gardens of the Great
  Mughals* (Plate XXIX), 94
Avantipur, 93

Babur, Zahīr-ud-Dīn Muhammad, 88
baby Taj (I'timad-ud-Daulah, tomb of),
  Agra, 104, 109
Bagge, Sir Alfred, 57
Baig, Abbas Ali, 138
Baker, Sir Herbert, 3, 85, 205
Bamba, HH Princess, 34
Baramulla, 131
Barcelona, 202–203
Barnard, Miss G.V., 230
Baroque, Spanish, 207, 210
Bayley, Sir Steuart, 137–138
Beachamwell Hall
  estate management, 54–57, 73,
    163–164, 216–217
  fire, 60, **64**
  gardens, 34, 67, 206–207, 220–222,
    231, 232
  honeymoon visit (Joshua and Frances),
    21–23
  house parties, 58
  painting room/studio, 67
  prints, **22**, **64**, **66**
  purchase by Fielden Trustees, 21
  relocation to, 29–35
  restoration and reconstruction, 60–67
  return to, post fire, 67
  sale of, 1967, 3
Begg, John, 87
Bermuda, 243–244
Between Zueluz & Sintra (1939,
  watercolour and pencil), **225**
Bharatpur
  HH the Maji Sahiba of, 88
  Lohagarh Fort, 168, **170**
Bhopal, Sultan Jahan Begum, 88, 110,
  167, 204
Bhownaggree, Sir Mancherjee, 166–167
Birdwood, Sir George, 87, 137, 139

Birkacre
    Company, 17, 19, 57
    Estate, 19, 27, 52
Birkbeck, Mrs E.W., 65
Bixley Hall, 65
Black, Adam, 163
Blicking Hall, Norfolk, 243
Blomfield, Reginald, 65
Bolton, 8, 15, 19
Bomanjee, Sir Dhunjibhoy, 167
Boston, Massachusetts, 240–242
Bovay, Miss (Constance's governess), 36
Bridge on SS Castalia (1911, pencil),
    79
Britain Can Make It (V&A exhibition,
    1945), 228–229
Brittany, 52–54
Bulgaria, 227
Burgh Hall, Birkacre estate, 19
Bush Fire in the Mundi Ranges (1889,
    watercolour), **49**

Cape Leeuwin, 42
Cape of Good Hope, 238
Cape Roca, 60
Cappoquin, County Waterford, 73
Cardale, Rear Admiral Hubert, 146
Casa Carmens, 202
Casa de Pesça, Deiras (1939, watercolour
    and pencil), **224**
Casa del Rey Morro, Ronda, 203
Castalia, SS, 77–79
Caton Green, 7, 9, 12
Chachrauli Palace, Karnal, 168
Chahol, Monsieur, 56
Charbagh (four waterways) garden design,
    86
Chasma Shah (Chashme Shahi), 126
Chatterton, John, 18
Chelmsford, Lady, 165–166
Chichester, the Hon. Claud, 74
Chorley, 21
Church of the Holy Apostles (1916, pencil
    and coloured crayon), 150, **154**
Cintra Foothills and Guincho Beach (1939,
    watercolour and pencil), **226**
Clifford, Lord de, 29, 34
Clock-Tower Mosque, The (1916, pencil
    and coloured crayon), 155, **157**

Cockcroft, Sarah, *see* Fielden, Sarah
    (Constance's grandmother)
Cockerell, Sir Sydney, 229
Cockley Cley Hall, Norfolk, 232
Colvin, Brenda, 228–229
Coming in from the Country (1916, pencil
    and coloured crayon), 155, **156**
Constance Fielden with her mother and
    unidentified aunts and uncles (1906,
    print), **72**
Constance Villiers Stuart and the Queen
    Mother (1952, print), **242**
Constance Villiers Stuart arranging
    flowers (*c.*1950, print), **236**
Constance Villiers Stuart in her garden
    (1911, print), **84**
Coolidge, Helen, 243
Coomaraswamy, Ananda, 141
Coombs, John, 51
Coral Beach Club, Bermuda, 244
Cordova, 189, 195, 204
cotton industry, 8
Countess of Dundonald's Hospital,
    Belgravia, 162
Country Life
    Baroque Garden of Casa Gomis, 1934
        article, 207
    Beachamwell hall feature, 206–207
    British Way of Life: A lead from
        Sweden in museum display, 1945
        article, 228, 230
    Constance's journalism, 140–141
    flower arranging, Constance's writings
        on, 235
    Future of Country House Gardens,
        1946 article, 207
    Gardens of the Great Mughals, review,
        137, 139
    Indian Garden Palaces, 1915 article,
        141
    Modern Trends in Flower Decoration,
        1959 article, 244
    Peterhoff: The Russian Versailles, 1957
        article, 245
    Photographed from an Aeroplane:
        Soldiers' Gardens, Salonica, 1916
        article, 158
    Portraits in the Landscape Park
        exhibition, 231

Three Kashmir Flowers, 1916 article, 161

County Hall, London, 231

Crown Imperial (flower), 131, 222

Culcheth New Hall, Bowden, 18

Cypress Steps, The (c.1927, drawing and lantern slide), **190**

Dal Lake (Lake of the Flowers), Srinigar, 101, 121–122, 126, 189

Darogha Bagh (Lalla Rookh's garden), 126

de Glehn, Wilfrid, 185–187

Deeg Palace, 141, 168–175

Delhi Durbar, 3, 102, 109–111

Dervish, Chief, in Constance's Times article, 162

Dilkusha Bagh, Shahdara, 93

Diver, Maud, 94

Diwan-i-'Am (public garden), Shalimar, 91, 115–118, **117**, **119**

Diwan-i-Khas, Chahrauli Palace, The (1924, watercolour), 168, **169**

Diwan-i-Khas (Hall of Private Audience), Red Fort, Delhi, 112, **113**

Diwan-i-Khas (private spaces), Shalimar, 91

Donald, French Colouring 20-cen (1929, watercolour), **214**

Dromana House, 73

Du Pont Gardens, Willington, Philadelphia, 243–244

dyes, natural, 19

Easter Lilies, 244

Eastern Daily Press, 230, 234, 238

École des Beaux Arts, 56

Edward, Prince of Wales (Edward VII), 21, 35

El Escorial, 189

El Labertino gardens, Horta, 189

El Retiro gardens, Madrid, 189

Elizabeth, Queen Mother and Queen Consort, 240

Elspeth, French Pastelists 18th Century Colouring (1929, watercolour), **212**

Evening in the Garden of the Taj, An (1911, watercolour), **106**

Evening Standard, 245

Fatehpur Sikri, 104

Fawcett, Millicent Garrett, 165

Fergusson, James, 87

Festival of the Roses, Kashmir, 122

Fielden brothers, 9–10, 27

Fielden, Constance, see Stuart, Constance Villiers

Fielden Family, The (1889, F B Mendelsohn & Co.), **47**

Fielden Family Trustees, 10, 12, 21

Fielden, Frances (Constance's mother)
    artistic talent, 2, 18–21, 29, 36–37, 46
    in Australia, 41–50
    background, 15
    character, 217
    on Constance's marriage, 71
    death of, 206, 216–217
    education, 18
    in Egypt, 36–40
    estate, management of, 54–57, 163, 216–217
    flower paintings, 29
    on foreigners, 40
    Joshua's death, impact of, 54–55
    journals, 28
    landscapes, 29, 36–37
    marriage, 21
    orientalist viewpoint, 38
    Patricia, care of, 75, 164
    sketch of Joshua, 19–21
    on slavery, 38

Fielden, John (Constance's grandfather), 12–13, 27

Fielden, Joshua (1748–1811), 8–9

Fielden, Joshua (1778–1847), 27

Fielden, Joshua (Constance's father)
    in Australia, 41–50
    birth, 12
    death of, 54–55
    disillusionment, 23
    drinking, 23, 43, 55
    education, 10
    financial situation, 10, 57
    as High Sheriff of Norfolk, 35
    marriage, 15, 21

Fielden, Mary (Constance's aunt), 12–13

Fielden, Sarah (Constance's grandmother), 12–15, 19, 220

Fitzwilliam Museum, Cambridge, 229

flower arranging, 220, 230–231, 234–240
flower festivals, Kashmir, 122
Flower Study 2 (1884, watercolour, Frances Fielden), **30**
Forestier, Jean Claude, 203
Fort, Bharatpure, The (1924, pencil), **170**
Fortnum and Mason, 142
Fountaine, Margaret, 58
Framfield Red, Rembrandt Colouring (1929, watercolour), **215**
Frémin, Jean, 191
Freud, Sigmund, 217–218
From the Atlantic Cliffs (1939, watercolour and pencil), **223**

Galerius, Emperor, 155
Gallipoli, 140, 227
Garden Club of America, 206
Garden Club of Bermuda, 243–244
Garden Museum, London, 6
gardens at Chasma Shah, Kashmir, the (1912, pencil), **127**
Gardens of the Great Mughals
    Achibal (Plate XXIX), 94, 99
    agenda of, 204–205, 232
    Agra from the Taj (Plate XII), 107
    alterations to, 135
    An Evening in the Gardens of the Taj (Plate V), 106
    cover, 122
    dedication, 134
    Diwan-i-'Am, Shalimar Bagh (Plate XXIII), 117
    Diwan-i-Khas, Delhi (Plate XVII), 112–113
    flowers in decorative art and symbolism, 238
    Great Waterfall, Achibal Bagh (Plate XXVIII), 100
    Hall of the Fountains (Plate XXV), 122–123
    idea for, 77–78
    images, selection of, 128
    Marble Swing, Deeg (Plate XXXVII), 176
    Octagonal Tank (Plate XXVII), 129–130
    Old Entrance, Shalimar Bagh (Plate XXII), 90

Patrick's enthusiasm for, 78
    Pinjor (Plate XXXII), 133
    publication, 135
    research for, 80, 83, 87–88
    reviews, 135–137, 139
    sales figures, 162–163
    Shah-Dara (Plate XIX), 92
    writing style, 202
Gardens of the Maids of Honour, Udaipur (1924, print), **177**
Gardeners' Chronicle, 136
Gates were as of Pearl, The (1911, watercolour), 102, **103**
Gaudi, Antoni, 203, 210
Generalife, Alhambra, Granada, 189, 198
George V, King of the United Kingdom, Emperor of India, 109–111, 182
George, Walter, 205
Gibralta, 60
Gloire À Notre France Eternelle (1916, print), **160**
Governor's House (Raj Bhavan), Srinagar, 126
Granada, 189, 195, 198, 204
Great Mosque, Cordova, 195
Great Waterfall, The (1911, pencil and watercolour), **100**
green spaces, 233
Greenbank, Caton Green, 12, 15, 21, 23, 28–29
Güell, Eusebi, 203
Gul-i-Mazar, Iris (flower of the graves), 122
Gupta, Sir Krishna, 138

Hake, Sir Henry, 229
Hall of Fountains, The (1912, watercolour and lantern slide), **123**, **124**
Hall of the Fountains, Nishat Bagh, 121–124
Hardinge, Lady, 3, 86, 112, 138, 165, 205, 232
Hardinge, Lord, 3, 86, 112, 118, 134–135, 232
Harrock Hill (c.1885, watercolour, Frances Fielden), **37**
Hart, Chichele Keppel, 58
Havell, E.B., 87, 104, 137–138

Healsville, Victoria, 46
Heptapyrgion, The, 148
Hird, Frank, 58
Hitler, Adolf, 218
Hobart, Richard, 243
Holding, Mrs Ursula, 189
Holy Wisdom (1916, pencil and coloured crayon), 150, **152**
Horta, 189
Horticultural Club, 137, 138–139
Hospital Number Four, Salonica (1916, print), 158, **159**
Hospital, The (1905, pencil and pastel), **69**
Hotel Splendide, Salonica, 147–148
Hudson, Edward, 206
Hussey, Christopher, 207
Huxley, Aldous, 94

ikebana, 238
Île St. Honorat (1882, watercolour, Frances Fielden), **31**
Ilex Wood, The (1900, pastel), **62**
In the Aviation Camp (1916, print), **160**
In the Garden (1905, pencil and pastel), **68**
In the Turkish Town, 148
Indian Mule Corps, Salonica, 158
Indian Women's Education Association (IWEA), 3, 165–168, 204
Institute of Landscape Architects (ILA), 5, 83, 135, 206, 229, 232, 234, 240
Interior (1911, watercolour), **76**
International Landscape Conference, 231
I'timad-ud-Daulah, gardens of the tomb, 104, 109

Jackson's Hotel, Jubbulpore, 80, **81–82**
Jahangir, Emperor, 91, 115, 126
Jain prince's garden, Jubbulpore, 86
Jaipur, 88, 171
Jammu and Kashmir, HH the Maharaja of, 115, 118
Japanese floral art, 238
Jebel Musa, 60
Jekyll, Gertrude, 6, 139
Jellicoe, Geoffrey, 232, 240
Jewish Town, Salonica, 148–150
Jones, Dr. Ernest, 218

Jubbulpore (Jabalpur), 78, 80–83, 85–86, 102, 232
Jullundur (Jalandhar), 168

kahwa (Kashmiri tea), 122
Karnal (Haryana), East Punjab, 168
Kashmir, 93–103, 114–131
King's Gardens (Tagore Gardens), Jubbulpore, 83, 85
Kodak cameras, 175
Kostorino, battle of, 143–144

La Granja (1925, watercolour), 191, **193**
La Granja gardens, 189–191
La Zubia, 202
Lady Hardinge Medical College, New Delhi, 167
Lahore, 80, 88–93
Lake Pichola, Udaipur (1924, print), **178**
Lalla Rookh, 93, 101, 126
Lancashire Landscape (c.1870, watercolour, Frances Fielden), **20**
Landscape Gardens Past and Present, Illustrated London News, 231
Lawley, Sir Arthur, 73
Lehzen, Baroness, 218
Lembet Camp, Salonica, 158
Liddar valley, 93
Limoges, 56
Lisbon, 238
Little Massingham House, 65
Livingstone, Dr. David, 18–19
Lolab valley, 126
Long Walk, Beachamwell Hall, The (1926, watercolour and prints), 207, **208–209,** 231
Lostock Grange, 15
lotus flowers, 89, 122, 126, 138, 162
Lotus Fountain, The (1925, watercolour and lantern slide), 198, **199–200**
Lower Pavilion (Hall of the Fountains), Nishat Bagh, **120,** 121–124
Lowestoft, housing exhibition, 233
Lutyens, Edwin, 3, 85, 138–139, 163, 204–205
Lytton, Lord and Lady, 166–167
Madeira, 67
Madrid, 189
Maison de la Duchesse Anne, Brittany, 54

Majorca, 189, 202
Manasbal, Lake, 93, 126
Marble Swing, Deeg, The (*c.*1900, print), **176**
Margate, 60, **61**
Martand, Sun Temple, 93–94, 98
Martin, Rita, 75
Mary, Princess, 166
Mary, Queen of the United Kingdom, Empress of India, 110, 134, 230
Mason, Mr Clacton, 56
Massachusetts Horticultural Society, Boston, 240
Maugham, Syrie, 238
Medina Azahara, 195
Melbourne, 43, 46
Metropolitan Museum of Art (The Met), New York, 244
Milbanke, Mark, 179–180
Molotov, SS, 245
Mond, Lady, 167
Montague Mansions, No.1, 75, **76**
Moore, Thomas, 101
More Flower Schemes, 238
Morlaix, 52–54
Mosley, Oswald, 218
Mount Pleasant House, Philadelphia, 243
Mount St Leonard, 46, **48**
Moynihan, Lisa, 245
Mundi hills, 46, **49**
Mustoe, William, 205

nader-monja (lotus stem fritters), 122
Naidu, Mrs Sarojini, 138
Nancy Smith of New York crossing the line, The (1888, watercolours), 43, **45**, 46
Nation and Atheneum, 204
National Portrait Gallery, 229
National Union of Women's Suffrage Societies, 165
Nedou's hotels, Srinagar and Gulmarg, 114
Nemon, Oscar, 206, 217–220, 246
New Delhi, 86–87, 112, 121, 134–135, 138–139, 167, 202, 204–205, 232
New York, 244
New York Times, 204
Newport, Rhode Island, 243

Nicol, Brigadier, 144
Nishat Bagh (Garden of Delights), 101, 114, 121–124, 141, 189
Nordiska Museet, Stockholm, 228, 230
North Entrance, Martand (1911, pencil sketch), **98**
North Foreland, Margate, Kent (1899, watercolour), **61**
Norwich Castle Museum, 229–231
Nur Jahan, Empress, 91, 109, 115, 126

Octagonal Tank, The (1913, Plate), **130**
Old Entrance, Shalimar Bagh, Lahore, The (1911, painting), **90**
Old Town, Salonica, 148–150
On the road to Avantipur (1911, watercolour sketches), **95–97**
On the Way to Shalimar (1912, watercolour), **116**
Ormanli, 144
Oxford and Buckinghamshire Light Infantry, 7th Battalion, 227

Pale Pink Crinum with Japanese Anemone leaves (c1955, print), **239**
Palice, Comtesse Marie de Chabannes, la, 147
Parc Güell, Barcelona, 203
Patio del Museo (1925, watercolour), 195, **196–197**
Pavilion of Charles V, The Alcázar (1925, watercolour), 198, **201**
Peet, Mary, *see* Thom, Mary (Constance's grandmother)
Pendleton, 15, 17
Persian paradise gardens, 118
Philadelphia, 243–244
Philip V, King of Spain, 191
Pilkington family, 13, 15
Pinjor Garden (Pinjore or Yadavindra Garden), 1, 114, 131–132, **133**
Pioneer, The, 136, 138
Pir Panjal mountains, 93
Piraeus, 146
Platt, Dr Kate, 167
Playford, Private, 142
Pompeii (1895, watercolour), 58, **59**
Pont-Aven school, 54
Port Said, 38

Portrait of Constance Fielden (J.E. Mayall), **25**

Portrait of Constance Villiers Stuart (1927, Vandyk Studio), **184**

Portrait of Frances Fielden (Unknown), **16**

Portrait of Joshua Fielden (S. Hallé), **11**

Portrait of Patricia and Constance Villiers Stuart (1918, Mark Milbanke), **180**

Portrait of Patricia Villiers Stuart (1922, Marcus Adams), **181**

Portrait of Patricia Villiers Stuart (1927, Vandyk Studio), **183**

Portrait of Patricia Villiers Stuart (1928, Wilfrid de Glehn), **186**

Portrait of Patricia Villiers Stuart (1930, Madame Yvonde), **188**

Portrait of Patrick Villiers Stuart (1905, print), **70**

Portrait of Sarah Fielden (Unknown), **14**

Portraits in the Landscape Park (Norwich Castle Museum exhibition), 230–231

prefabricated houses, 233

Purdah system, 86, 167

Queen magazine, 229

Queen's *hindola* (swing), Deeg Palace, 175

Quimper cap, 53

Rajput Painting (Coomaraswamy), 141

Ram Bagh, Agra, 104

Raxa, Majorca, 189, **190**

Read, Mr, 56

Red and Pink Geraniums with Red Monarda (*c*.1955, print), **241**

Red Cross, 158, 162

Red Door, Suraj Bhawan, Deeg, The (1924, watercolour), 171, **172–173**

Red Fort, Delhi, 112

Red Pillar, The (1916, pencil and coloured crayon), 150, **153**

Red Star, Lely Colour Scheme (1929, watercolour), **211**

Review of Reviews, 203

Riviera, the, 2, 74

Rocks at Heysham (*c*.1885, watercolour, Frances Fielden), **37**

Ronda, 203

Royal Academy, 233

Royal Academy of Arts, 139

Royal Free Hospital, 166

Royal Fusiliers, 2nd Battalion, 73–74, 102, 140, 142–143, 168, 227

Royal Fusiliers Chronicle, 136

Royal Institute of British Architects, 204

Royal Society of Arts (RSA), 137–138, 204

rural regeneration, 234

Sagrada Familia, 210

Salerno, 58

Salford, 15

Salonica, 144–158, 222, 227

Salonica, untitled (1916, pencil and coloured crayon), **151**

San Ildefonsa, 189

Sandringham Estate, 21, 35, 240

Scotney Castle, 207

Season, The, 185

Segovia, 189

Self-Portrait (1905, watercolour), **63**

Shah-Dara (1911, painting), **92**

Shahdara garden, 91–93

Shalimar Bagh (Abode of Love), 88–91, 101, 114–121, 141

shikara (Kashmiri boat), 121

Shimla (Simla), 114, 131

Shingham House, 60

Ship Billiards (1911, pencil), **79**

Ship's Flags on Sobraon (1888, watercolour), **44**

Side Street, Salonique in the Jewish Town, A (1916, pencil and coloured crayon), 148, **149**

Sikandra, Akbar's tomb, 104

Singh, Bhupinder, Maharaja of Patiala, 132

Singh, HH Princess Bamba Duleep, 88

Singh, Maharaja Duleep, 34

Singh, Maharaja Ravisher, 168

Singh, Prince Frederick Duleep, 138

Singh, Princess Sophia Duleep, 138, 167

Sketch of Irises on Unmarked Kashmiri Graves (1912, pencil), **125**

soap business, 15, 17

Sobraon (ship), 42–44

Somerset Club, Boston, 243

sons (properties) of Majorca, 202, 204
Sopore, 93, 126
Sorrento, 58
Spanish Gardens: Their History, Types and Features
fountains of Generalife (Plate XVIII), 198
idea behind, 164
Patio del Museo, Cordova (Plate XL), 195–197
Pavilion of Charles V (Plate I), 198
photography, 175, 187–189
promotion of, 207–208
publication and reviews, 203–204
research for, 187–189
style and organisation, 198, 202
Spring at La Granja (1925, watercolour), 191, **192**
Spry, Constance, 229, 235
Srinagar, 3, 93, 101, 114, 118, 126, 148
St George's Church, Chorley, 21
St Marguerite (1884, watercolour, Frances Fielden), **32**
St Mary's Church, Beachamwell, 246–247
St Paul's Church, Knightsbridge, 73
St Petersburg, 245
Stein, Sir Aurel, 87
Steps to the Upper Palace, Amber (1924, pencil), 171, **174**
Stuart, Constance Villiers
in Agra, 102–109
alchohol, attitude to, 55
archives of, 1–2, 5–6
artistic development, 3, 58, 60, 67, 210–216, 222
in Australia, 41–50
Beachamwell Hall reconstruction, role in, 60–67
in Bermuda, 244
birth, 23
on British garden design in India, 83, 85–87
in Brittany, 52–54
character, 23, 41, 89–91, 131, 162, 185
childhood, 23–27
death, 246
in Delhi, 109–113
education, 56

elitist attitudes, modification of, 231, 233
engagement to Patrick, 67
fashion, love of, 24, 53–54, 71, **72**
father's death, impact of, 54–55
as Fellow of ILA, 232
flower arranging, 220, 230–231, 234–240
honeymoon, Riviera, 74
in India, 1924 visit, 168–175
Indian traditions, respect for, 83, 85, 111
in Italy, 58
John Thom, influence of, 52
journalism, 140–141, 155–162, 207–208, 210, 227–228, 238–240
in Jubbulpore, 78, 80–83, 85–86
in Kashmir, 3, 93–103, 114–131
on Kashmiris, 128, 131
in Lahore, 88–93
as lecturer, 137–138, 139, 240–244
in Madeira, 67
oral cancer, 246
on Oscar Nemon, 217–220
Patricia, relationship with, 179–187, 206, 217–220, 227
Patrick, relationship with, 71–73, 139, 147, 164, 217
photography, 3, 88, 104, 175, 216, 234
Portraits in the Landscape Park exhibition, 230–231
in Portugal, 220–222
post-war hiatus, 164
pregnancy, 74–75
in Rajputana, 171–175
relocation to Beachamwell Hall, 34
as researcher, 87
return to England from India, 132
RSA silver medal, award of, 139
in Russia, 245
in Salonica, 140–141, 144–158
sketchbooks, Australia, 43, 46–50
sketchbooks, India, 80, 115, 127, 168, 171
sketchbooks, Spain, 191
still-life paintings, 210–216, 222
on town planning, 232–234
as traveller, 88

in USA, 240–244
wealth, 54–55
wedding, 73–74
Stuart, Gerald Villiers, 141
Stuart, Mary Villiers, 71
Stuart, Patricia Mary Villiers
    birth, 75
    childhood, 179
    Constance, breach with, 219–220,
        227
    on Constance's illnesses, 246
    as debutante, 182–187
    mental health, 217–218
    Oscar Nemon, relationship with,
        217–220
    pregnancy, 219
Stuart, Patrick Villiers
    background, 73
    Beachamwell estate, management of,
        73, 163–164
    character, 217, 227
    Constance, relationship with, 71, 139,
        147, 164, 217
    death of, 206, 222, 227
    engagement, 67
    in Gallipoli, 140
    India, posting to, 74
    in Kashmir, 94, 101–102, 114
    letters home, from Macedonian front,
        142–144
    mention in dispatches, 144
    Milbanke portrait, hatred of, 179
    in Salonica, 140–144
Study of Flowers (1884, watercolour), **26**
Sunday Times, Spanish Gardens review,
    203
Suraj Bhawan, 168, 171–172
Suraj Mal, 168, 175
Swaffham, 21
Sykes, Brigadier-General Sir Percy
    Molesworth, 118
Sylvia Slade, Holbein Colouring (1929,
    watercolour), **213**

Tagore Gardens, Jubbulpore, 83, 85
Taj Mahal, 102–108
Talkatora Bagh, Delhi, 118–120
Tasmania, SS, 38, 40
Tate Gallery, 233

Temple, Sir Richard, 138
Thierry, René, 191
Thom, Alfred, 18, 52
Thom, David, 15, 17
Thom, Frances, *see* Fielden, Frances
    (Constance's mother)
Thom, Harry, 17
Thom, John (Constance's grandfather),
    15, 17–19, 23, 51–52
Thom, Marion, 38, 52
Thom, Mary (Constance's grandmother),
    17–18
Thom, Walter, 52
Times Literary Supplement, 136, 203
Times of India, 166
Times, The
    Constance's 'At Home' for the Lyttons,
        166
    Constance's Salonica article, 1917,
        161–162
    Portraits in the Landscape Park
        exhibition, 231
Tipping, H. Avray, 206
Todmorden, 12
Torre Güell, Barcelona, 202–203
tourism industry, 28–29
Trefusis, Lady Mary, 134
Trustees, Fielden Family, 10, 12, 21
Turner, Mr. (Head Gardener,
    Beachamwell Hall), 220, **221**

Udaipur, 88, 171, 175, 177–178
Umayyad dynasty, 195
Umballa (Ambala), 132
Upcher, Edith, 73

Vandyk, Carl, 182
Vandyk, Hubert, 182
Verinag Bagh, 93, 115, 126–128
Via Egnatia, 161
Viceroy's House (Rashtrapti Bhavan),
    New Delhi, 3, 86–88, 112, 118, 134,
    139, 204–205, 232
Victoria and Albert Museum, 137, 228
Victoria, Queen of the United Kingdom,
    Empress of India, 21, 182, 218
Village near Castiglione (1882,
    watercolour, Frances Fielden), **33**
Villiers, Major, Provost Marshal, 146

Viznar, Archbishop's Palace, 202
Volo (Volos), 146

Wharton Crags (*c.*1885, watercolour,
    Frances Fielden), **37**
White and Green Scheme with Arum Lilies
    (*c.*1955, print), **237**
White Tower, Salonica, 150
Willingdon, Lady, 165
Wimperis and Best, 65–66
Woman feeding Fish at Verinag Bagh
    (1912, watercolour), **129**

Women's Journal, 187
Woodall, Lt. Gen. Sir John and Lady
    Woodall, 244
Wooden Eaves, Salonica (1916, pencil and
    coloured crayon), **145**
World Monument Fund, 109
Wular, Lake, 93, 126

Yarra valley, 46
Yvonde, Madame, 187

Zafar, Bahadur Shah, Emperor, 112